中国长城示意图

Sketch Map of the Great Wall

乌鲁木齐
Urumqi

玉门关
Yumenguan Pass

敦煌
Dunhuang

嘉峪关
Jiayuguan Pass

酒泉
Jiuquan

张掖
Zhangye

武威
Wuwei

西宁
Xining

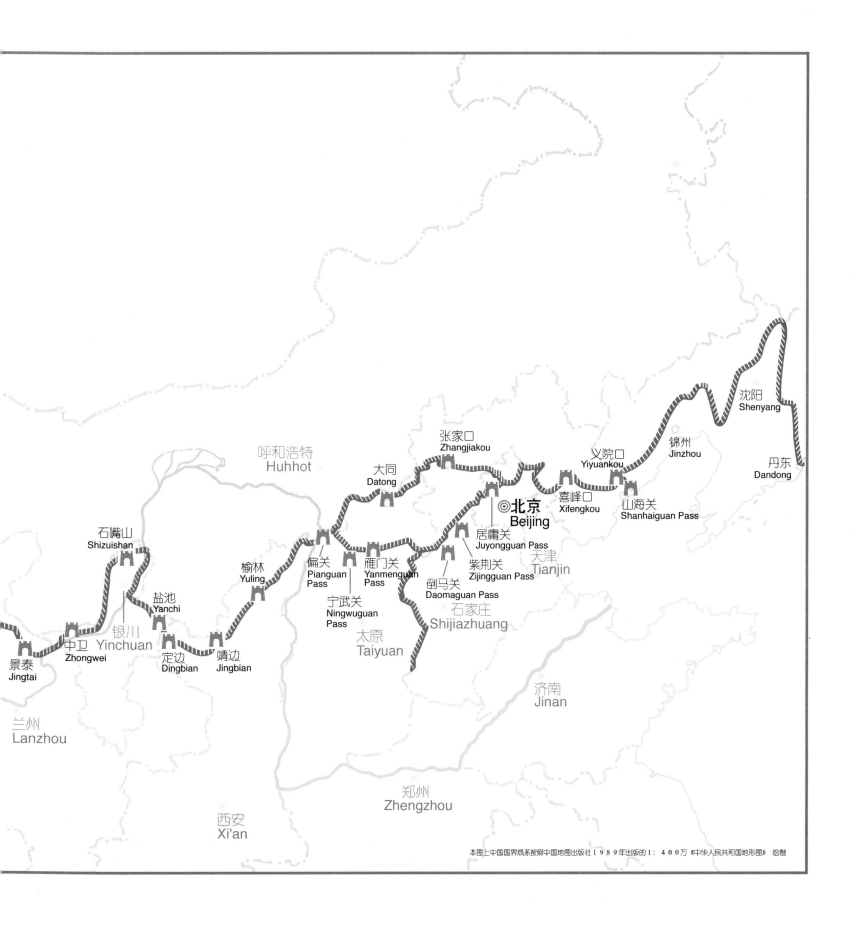

张家口
Zhangjiakou

沈阳
Shenyang

义院口
Yiyuankou

锦州
Jinzhou

丹东
Dandong

呼和浩特
Huhhot

大同
Datong

◎北京
Beijing

喜峰口
Xifengkou

山海关
Shanhaiguan Pass

石嘴山
Shizuishan

居庸关
Juyongguan Pass

天津
Tianjin

榆林
Yuling

偏关
Pianguan
Pass

雁门关
Yanmenguan
Pass

紫荆关
Zijingguan Pass

盐池
Yanchi

宁武关
Ningwuguan
Pass

倒马关
Daomaguan Pass

石家庄
Shijiazhuang

银川
Yinchuan

太原
Taiyuan

中卫
Zhongwei

定边
Dingbian

靖边
Jingbian

景泰
Jingtai

济南
Jinan

兰州
Lanzhou

郑州
Zhengzhou

西安
Xi'an

本图上中国国界线系按照中国地图出版社1989年出版的1：400万《中华人民共和国地形图》绘制

万里の長城

THE GREAT WALL
LA GRANDE MURAILLE
DIE GROSSE MAUER

新世界出版社
New World Press

An Introduction to the Great Wall of China

The Great Wall is in fact made up of many walls sprawling across northern China from the Yalu River in the east to Jiayuguan Pass in Gansu Province in the west. Combined, the various segments of the wall span some 10,000 *li* (over 6,300 kilometers) across the provinces of Hebei, Shanxi, Shaanxi, and Gansu, the Ningxia Hui and Inner Mongolia autonomous regions, and the Beijing Municipality. Although the wall proved inadequate to stop the organized and systematic invasions from the north that led to the founding of the Yuan and Qing dynasties, the tangible barrier presented by the wall was enough to limit any cross-border raids by small parties, and therefore was instrumental in protecting the northern regions of the Chinese empire during periods of feudal strength. The wall has been likened to a dragon winding from the east to the west through deserts, valleys, and mountain passes. The dragon's head bows into the ocean waters in the east and the dragon's tail settles in the parched earth of Gansu Province. Along the course of the wall are natural mountain passes and valleys that would have allowed access to the empire from the north. Hundreds of these passes were fortified and some fortifications survive today. Beacon towers were constructed at vantage-points and were used to send up the alarm when military movements were seen beyond the wall. At night the beacon fires could be seen from one beacon tower to the next. During the day, wolf's feces was added to the fire because it would produce a thick black smoke that could clearly be seen even on a cloudy day.

The number of fires lit by the troops on the beacon tower would provide a clue as to how many troops were amassing outside the frontier. According to military regulations set down in 1466, one fire would be lit and one cannon shot fired to warn of the approach of a force numbering less than 500 soldiers. If an army of 500 to 1,000 approached, two fires would be lit and two cannon shots fired; for 1,000 to 5,000, three fires and three cannon shots; for 5,000 to 10,000, four fires and four cannon shots; and for an army that surpassed 10,000 the troops would light five fires and fire off five cannon shots as a warning. In this way, the garrison commander not only knew from which direction the enemy was advancing, but knew how large a force he would have to deal with. In ancient times, the main weapons of an army were swords, arrows, and spears. This type of combat required armies to close upon each other. The barrier presented by the Great Wall played an important strategic role in limiting the need for Chinese soldiers to frequently close on enemy groups. If the force was not strong enough to breach the Great Wall fortifications, then it may not have been necessary for the Chinese soldiers to make contact with the enemy army.

Many segments of the Great Wall were built along steep ridgelines and plunging valley walls. Today, many visitors to the wall find it a daunting task to climb these sections even unhindered. They cannot imagine the difficulties involved in actually building the wall in these areas. The stone blocks used to construct the Badaling section of the Great Wall weigh over one tonne each. When this section was first built, the only construction tools available were human hands and backs and the most basic block-and-tackle technologies. A stone tablet dated 1582, during the Ming Dynasty, records the construction of a 200-meter section of the wall. This small project required several thousand garrison troops and a great number of conscripted laborers and took an entire year to complete.

Construction of the Great Wall can be traced to the Spring and Autumn Period (770-256 BC) and the Warring States Period (475-221 BC). During these periods, local warlords vied for supremacy, and conflict was a nearly constant element of life. Warlords built massive city walls to protect their personal holdings. This concept was expanded to include the entire area under their control and they began to construct walls along their borders as a way of defending their limited domains. These walls were the precursors of the Great Wall we see today. In 221 BC, Qin Shi Huang defeated several powerful warlords and united the Han people of the Yellow River Valley as one nation. He founded the Qin Dynasty, the first to unite China. In order to protect the new empire from the nomads of the northern steppes, Qin Shi Huang ordered the existing walls built by the Qin, Zhao, and Yan kingdoms in the north to be united as one barrier. The Qin Dynasty Great Wall begins in Lintao, Min County in Gansu Province and travels east to the Liaodong Peninsula.

Because the Qin Dynasty Great Wall connected over 10,000 *li* of walls, beacon towers, and passes, it has been called the "10,000-*li* Great Wall".

When the Qin Dynasty collapsed after only 100 years, the Han Dynasty replaced it. The Han Dynasty (206 BC-AD 220) undertook a massive construction project to repair and fortify the Great Wall. The Han Dynasty Great Wall was extended another 5,000 kilometers to the west and reached the Lop Nur Lake in today's Xinjiang Uygur Autonomous Region. Subsequent dynasties took similar stands in regard to the defensive value of the Great Wall.

Even after the Ming Dynasty (1368-1644) had brought the Yuan Dynasty (1271-1368) to an end and pushed the Mongols beyond the Great Wall, the Mongols continued to harass the areas along the northern frontier. During the final century of the Ming Dynasty, the nomads of Manchuria founded a settled kingdom and began to expand their power sphere to the south. The combination of continued conflict along the border with Mongolia and new problems in the northeast posed serious threats to the Ming rulers. As a response, the Ming court ordered the renovation and restoration of the Great Wall. For nearly 200 years, work continued on the wall. What we see today is primarily the remnants of the Ming Dynasty Great Wall.

Although 2,000 years of efforts by some 20 kingdoms and dynasties were aimed at creating an impenetrable barrier against invasions, the 50,000 kilometers of the Great Wall have given up their defensive value to become a symbol of the ingenuity, skill, strength, and dedication of the Chinese nation.

航空遥感图上的万里长城

A section of the Great Wall of China captured by satellite imaging.

写真は、リモートセンシングによる航空写真がとらえた万里の長城。

La Grande Muraille,téléphotographiée par le satellite.

Satellitenaufnahme der Großen Mauer

统一中国的秦始皇
A portrait of the founder of the Qin Dynasty, the Emperor Qin Shi Huang, who ordered the scattered walls built by warlords to be linked into one great wall.

中国を統一した秦の始皇帝
Portrait de l'empereur Shihuangdi des Qin.

Qin Shi Huang, Erster Kaiser der Qin-Dynastie

秦、汉、隋、金长城遗址　金长城采用掘地为壕，垒土打夯成墙。金修筑长城也长达一万华里。

Ruins of the Great Wall dating to different periods. Top to bottom, Qin Dynasty, Han Dynasty, Sui Dynasty, Jin Dynasty. The Jin Dynasty Great Wall was 5,000 kilometers of packed earthen mounds.

秦、漢、隋、金の四王朝の長城の遺跡　金代の長城は、外側は黄土を積み上げた壁で囲み、壁の中の地面を掘り下げたうえで土を打ち固めたものである。金代の長城の長さは10000余華里にもおよんでいる。

Les ruines des murailles construites sous les règnes des Qin, des Han, des Sui et des Jin. La muraille en pisé des Jin avait une longueur de 5000 km.

Die Ruinen der Großen Mauer aus der Qin-, Han-, Sui- und Jin-Dynastie Die Lehmmauer aus der Jin-Dynastie war 10 000 Li (5000 km) lang.

万里长城

　　万里长城位于中国北部，东起辽宁省鸭绿江畔，西至甘肃省的嘉峪关，横跨河北、北京、山西、内蒙古、宁夏、陕西、甘肃等七个省、市、自治区，长约一万二千七百余华里（六千三百余公里），故称"万里长城"。

　　长城是中国古代坚固的军事防御工事，犹如一条巨龙，蜿蜒越过无数高山峻岭，穿过莽莽草原和浩瀚大漠，连接百座雄关、隘口。在长城上或长城内外群山制高点上，修有成千上万座敌台和烽火烟墩。一处望敌入侵，白天燃狼粪，狼烟腾空不散，很远就能看见；夜晚举火把，火光更是显而易见；还要根据来犯敌军多寡燃点烟堆、火把数量。如明朝成化二年（公元1466年）规定：来敌人数百人，举一烟，鸣炮一响；来敌五百，两烟两炮；来敌千人，三烟三炮；来敌五千，四烟四炮；来敌万人，五烟五炮。以此数类推燃烟、鸣炮，处处烽火台、烟墩遥相呼应，迅速将敌情传到指挥部和京城朝廷。这样，指挥官不仅知道敌人从何处来，还知道敌人来了多少，就能迅速派兵增援。这在以大刀、长矛、弓箭为武器的作战古代，长城在抵御外敌来犯上，发挥了重要作用。

　　长城沿山脊险峰修筑，坡度异常陡峭，游人徒手登城还气喘嘘嘘，要运送几米长、上千公斤重的大石砌长城，在没有运输工具的年代，其困难可想而知。在八达岭长城上发现一块明朝石碑，记载了万历十年（公元1582年），用几千军兵加上众多民夫，才能修筑起200米长一小段长城，可见修长城之难。

　　中国古代修建长城最早要追溯到春秋战国时代（公元前770-前221年）。那是诸侯纷争的年代。各诸侯国为了互相防御对方攻城夺地，各自在自己的领地上修建了城墙，称之为长城。这即是万里长城的前身。公元前221年，秦始皇统一了中国。他为了防御北方游牧民族南下骚扰、侵犯，命令将原来的秦、赵、燕等各诸侯国建在北方的长城加以联结和延长。它西起临洮（今甘肃省岷县），东直辽东，长达一万余华里，形成中国第一条"万里长城"，称之为秦长城。

　　秦灭汉兴。汉王朝（公元前206-公元220年）认识到长城防御的重要性，大规模修建长城。将秦长城沿丝绸之路从酒泉经敦煌直至新疆罗布泊以西延伸，长达两万余华里，称之为汉长城。

　　明朝（公元1368-1644年）为抵御蒙古贵族不断南下骚扰，还要防止女真政权崛起入侵，修建长城长达二百余年，这就是我们今天所见到的长城，史学家称之为明长城。

　　两千多年来，中国有二十多个诸侯国和封建王朝修筑过长城，总长约五万余公里。今天，万里长城成为世界七大奇迹之一。它作为防御工事已完成了它的历史使命，但作为中国古代文化的象征，还将长期地横亘在地球上。

　　本画册在编辑过程中得到外文出版社的大力支持，这里表示感谢！

まえがき

　　万里の長城は中国の北部に位置している。東は遼寧省の鴨緑江を起点とし、西は甘粛省の嘉峪関に至り、河北、北京、山西、内蒙古、寧夏、陝西、甘粛など七省・市・自治区にまたがり、全長１２７００余華里（６３００余キロ）で、それゆえに「万里の長城」と呼ばれている。

　　万里の長城は中国古代の堅固な軍事防御施設で、巨竜のように起伏した山峰をに沿って曲がりくねって延々と連なり、茫々たる草原と広大な砂漠を通り抜け、数百の関所、要塞がある。長城の城壁の上あるいは長城の内側と外側の起伏する群山の最高所には幾千幾万ののろし台があり、敵情を知らせるためのものであった。昼間はオオカミの糞を燃やし、煙が空高く上がって消え去らず、遠くから見やすくなっている。夜はタイマツをともし、炎の光はだれの目にもはっきり見てとれた。このほか、敵の人数に応じて、煙の本数をきめたのである。たとえば、明の成化二年（西暦１４６６年）の頃は、規定によって、１００人前後の敵が襲来すると、煙を１本たてると同時に、大砲を１発放ったのである。５００人ならば、煙が２本、大砲が２発、１０００人以上ならば３本、３発、５０００人以上だと４本、４発、１００００人以上だったら５本、５発と、その他の場合もこの比例で類推することができる。のろし台とのろし台は互いに呼応しあって、敵情を急速に指揮所および宮廷に知らせることになっていた。こうすれば、敵の人数、侵入の方向はいつ、いかなるときでも把握することができ、そして軍隊を上手に指揮することができた。刀、矛、弓などの武器で戦った古代において、長城は軍事防御の面で重要な役割を果たした。

　　万里の長城はほとんど山の頂上に築かれ、地勢が高く険しい。観光客は徒手でさえ息をせききらせながら長城に登るのに、長さ何メートル、重さ何千キログラムの巨大な石を山の頂上へ運ぶのであるから、運搬手段が足りなかった時代においては、そのむずかしさは推して知るべしである。山の頂上では明代の造りである石碑が発見されている。石碑には、万暦十年（西暦１５８２年）、２００メートル余りの長城を築造するのに千名の兵士と人夫が必要だったということが刻まれている。このことから見ても長城の築造はたいへんむずかしかったことがわかる。

　　中国でははやくも春秋戦国時代（西暦前７７０年～西暦前２２１年）に長城が築かれた。それは各諸侯国間の紛争が絶えなかった時代であった。各諸侯国は防御のために、それぞれ自分の領土に城壁を築き、長城と称した。この長城はすなわち万里の長城の前身である。西暦前２２１年に、秦の始皇帝が中国を統一した。秦の始皇帝は北方遊牧民族の侵入を防ぐために、各諸侯国のつくった長城を結びつけ、それをさらに延長し、西は臨洮（今の甘粛省の岷県）から東は遼東に至る全長１００００余華里の防御線とし、秦代の長城と称した。

　　秦が滅されたあと、劉邦が漢の王朝をうちたてた。漢王朝（西暦前２０６年～西暦前２２０年）は大がかりな長城の築造に取り組んだ。秦のつくった長城に結びつけ、漢代の長城の西部はシルクロードに沿って酒泉から敦煌を経てロプノール湖に至り、全長２００００余華里で、漢代の長城と称された。

　　明王朝（西暦１３６８年～西暦１６４４年）は蒙古族および女真族の侵入に備えるために、長城を築いた。この長城の築造は２００余年にわたった。これは現代の人たちが目にすることのできる長城である。歴史学者はそれを「明代の長城」と呼んでいる。

　　２０００余年来、２０余りの諸侯国と封建王朝が長城の築造に取り組んだ。そのうち各王朝のつくった長城の長さはあわせて５００００余キロになる。今や万里の長城は世界の七大奇跡の一つとなっている。今日、かつては防御工事であった長城はすでにその歴史的使命を果たし終え、中国文化のシンボルとして、その姿を誇示している。

INTRODUCTION

Dans le nord de la Chine, la Grande Muraille part du fleuve Yalu à l'est et court vers l'ouest pour atteindre, au bout de 6 300 km, la Passe Jiayuguan, son terme, après avoir traversé le Hebei, Beijing, le Shanxi, la Mongolie intérieure, le Shaanxi, le Ningxia et le Gansu.

La Grande Muraille, gigantesque ouvrage de défense de la Chine antique, comporte une centaine de passes, et une dizaine de milliers de tours de guet et de feu d'alarme qui servaient à transmettre des messages ou des signaux militaires. À l'approche de l'ennemi, on y faisait monter, selon le cas, un nombre différent de colonnes de fumée, le jour, alors que des flammes étaient allumées la nuit. Par exemple, sous la dynastie des Ming, pour signaler une attaque de cent soldats, on allumait un feu et tirait une salve; pour cinq cents ennemis, deux feux et deux salves; trois pour un millier; quatre pour cinq mille; et cinq pour dix mille. Ainsi les renseignements ne tardaient-ils pas à parvenir à la capitale ou au quartier général de l'armée, qui disposait ses forces en conséquence. À l'époque où l'on combattait au sabre, à la lance et à l'arc, la Grande Muraille joua un rôle important dans la résistance à l'ennemi.

La Grande Muraille serpente, comme un dragon géant, sur les crêtes de montagnes escarpées à perte de vue. Sa construction fut extrêmement difficile par manque de moyens de transport. On trouve, sur le tronçon de la Grande Muraille à Badaling, près de Beijing, une stèle qui rapporte que l'empereur Wan Li des Ming mobilisa des milliers de soldats et de nombreux civils pour construire 200 m de muraille.

Les premières sections datent de l'époque des Printemps et Automnes (770-221 av. J.-C.) où les principautés qui guerroyaient construisaient des murailles pour défendre leur territoire. Après avoir unifié la Chine, l'empereur Shihuangdi des Qin fit relier les murailles construites par les États de Yan, Zhao et Qin, et construire de nouveaux tronçons pour se mettre à l'abri de l'invasion de tribus nomades du nord. Cette nouvelle ligne de défense, depuis Lintao (aujourd'hui district de Minxian au Gansu) à l'ouest jusqu'au Liaoning à l'est, totalisait une longueur de 5 000 km. On l'appelait la Grande Muraille des Qin. Sous les Han (206 av.J.-C.-220), cette muraille fut prolongée sur plus de 500 km vers l'ouest, le long de la Route de la Soie, jusqu'à Lob Nor. C'était la Grande Muraille des Han. Sous la dynastie des Ming (1368-1644), pour se défendre contre un éventuel retour des Mongols qui venaient d'être renversés, l'empereur ordonna de reconstruire la muraille. Les travaux durèrent 200 ans. C'est là la Grande Muraille que nous voyons aujourd'hui.

Durant plus de deux millénaires, la Grande Muraille fut érigée par une vingtaine de principautés et de dynasties féodales. L'ensemble des sections construites à différentes époques totalisait 50 000 km. Tous les chiffres montrent que cet ouvrage gigantesque est unique au monde. De nos jours, la Grande Muraille n'est plus une ligne de défense, mais le symbole de la civilisation de la Chine ancienne et une des sept merveilles du monde. Elle durera tant que durera notre planète.

Die Große Mauer

Die Große Mauer erstreckt sich von der Mündung des Yalu-Flusses in der Provinz Liaoning im Osten über Hebei, Beijing, Shanxi, die Innere Mongolei, Ningxia und Gansu bis zum Jiayuguan-Paß in der Provinz Gansu im Westen. Ihre Gesamtlänge beträgt über 12 700 Li (2 Li = 1 km). Deshalb heißt sie „Mauer mit einer Länge von 10 000 Li".

Die Große Mauer diente im alten China als Verteidigungsanlage. Die Mauerwände ziehen sich wie ein gigantischer Drache über hohe Berge und tiefe Täler, ausgedehnte Steppen und Wüsten und verbinden einige hundert Gebirgspässe und zehntausend Alarmfeuertürme sowie Wachtürme. Die Alarmfeuertürme wurden entlang bzw. innerhalb und außerhalb der Großen Mauer in bestimmten Abständen gebaut. Sie stehen meistens auf höher gelegenen Stellen. Im flachen Gelände haben sie ein weites Blickfeld. Kam es zu einem feindlichen Angriff, so signalisierten sie am Tag durch den Rauch von verbranntem Wolfskot und in der Nacht durch Feuerfackeln ihre Nachrichten. Außerdem wurde je nach der Anzahl der Angreifer eine bestimmte Zahl von Rauchsäulen oder Feuerfackeln festgesetzt, die abgebrannt werden mußten, z. B., im 2. Jahr der Regierungszeit des Kaisers Chenghua der Ming-Dynastie (1466) wurde festgelegt: Eine Rauchsäule und ein Schuß sollten etwa 100 Feinde melden, zwei Rauchsäulen und zwei Schüsse etwa 500 Feinde, drei Rauchsäulen und drei Schüsse über 1000 Feinde, vier Rauchsäulen und vier Schüsse über 5000 Feinde und fünf Rauchsäulen und fünf Schüsse über 10 000 Feinde. Auf diese Weise konnte eine Meldung von Turm zu Turm bis zur Verteidigungszone und Hauptstadt weitergeleitet werden. Dadurch wußten die betreffenden Kommandanten nicht nur Bescheid, woher die feindlichen Truppen kamen, sondern auch über deren Stärke. So konnten sie ihre Truppen und ihre Verstärkung richtig einsetzen. In alten Zeiten, in denen man mit Schwertern, Speeren, Pfeil und Bogen Kriege führte, spielte die Große Mauer im Widerstand gegen Angriffe der Feinde eine bedeutende Rolle.

Da die Große Mauer sich auf äußerst steilen Bergkämmen und Gipfeln schlängelt, wird sie von Touristen gerne besucht. Dabei müssen die Besucher teilweise extreme Höhenunterschiede zu Fuß bewältigen. Es ist kaum vorstellbar, wie die Menschen es zu jener Zeit schafften, wo keine modernen Transportmittel zur Verfügung standen, so viele große Steine anzuschleppen. Auf einer Steintafel aus der Ming-Dynastie, die in Badaling entdeckt wurde, ist die Inschrift zu lesen: Die Mauer wurde Stück für Stück von Grenzsoldaten und Bauern gebaut. Der Bau eines 200 m langen Mauerabschnitts nahm einige tausend Soldaten und eine Unzahl von Bauern in Anspruch.

Der Bau der Großen Mauer geht bis in die Zeit der Frühlings- und Herbstperiode und der Streitenden Reiche (770 -221 v. Chr.) zurück. Damals gerieten die Fürstentümer wie Qin, Zhao und Yan in Streit. Sie bauten zur Verteidigung ihrer eigenen Territorien jeweils Schutzmauern; diese Mauern waren die Vorläufer der Großen Mauer. 221 v. Chr. einigte Qin Shi Huang, Erster Kaiser der Qin-Dynastie, China. Um die Normadenstämme auf ihrem Weg von Norden nach Süden zu behindern, ließ er die einzelnen Mauern aus den Fürstentümern Qin, Zhao, Yan usw. verbinden und ausbauen. Zu jener Zeit begann die Große Mauer im Westen bei Lintao (heute Kreis Minxiang in der Provinz Gansu) und endete im Osten in der heutigen Provinz Liaoning. Sie erstreckte sich über mehr als 10 000 Li. Deshalb bezeichnete man sie auch die „Mauer mit einer Länge von 10 000 Li" oder die „Große Mauer der Qin-Dynastie".

Die Qin-Dynastie wurde bald durch die Han-Dynastie (206-220 n. Chr.) ersetzt. Da die Han-Herrscher die wichtige Rolle der Großen Mauer als Verteidigungsanlage erkannten, ließen sie die Große Mauer entlang der Seidenstraße weiter nach Westen verlängern, und zwar von Jiuquan über Dunhuang bis nach Lop Nur im heutigen Uigurischen Autonomen Gebiet Xinjiang. Ihre Gesamtlänge betrug über 20 000 Li, man nennt sie auch die „Große Mauer der Han-Dynastie".

Zur Abwehr gegen Störaktionen der mongolischen Adligen aus dem Norden und die Überfälle der Nüzhen-Macht wurde die Große Mauer in der Ming-Dynastie (1368-1644) über 200 Jahre lang weiter restauriert und ausgebaut. Das Ergebnis ist die Große Mauer, die wir heute kennen und Historiker als die „Große Mauer der Ming-Dynastie" bezeichnen

Das heißt, seit mehr als 2000 Jahren arbeiteten über 20 Fürstentümer und feudale Dynastien am Bau und an der Restaurierung der Großen Mauer, deren Gesamtlänge insgesamt ca. 50 000 km betrug. Heutzutage ist die Große Mauer eines der sieben Weltwunder. Sie hat als Verteidigungsanlage ihre historische Aufgabe vor einigen Jahrhunderten erfüllt, wird aber als Kultursymbol Chinas der Welt herhalten bleiben.

This illustration from the Ming Dynasty shows how the massive defensive walls were constructed.

写真は、中国古代の長城の築造に取り組んでいる模様。

Tableau décrivant la construction de la Grande Muraille.

Szene vom Bau der Großen Mauer im alten China

明代进入嘉峪关关门的 "令牌"

This command tablet was a symbol of imperial authority for the commander of the garrison troops stationed along the Great Wall around the Jiayuguan Pass.

写真は、嘉峪関から出入りするときに用いられた明代の "令牌（許可証みたいなもの）"。

Plaque de laissez-passer pour la Passe Jiayuguan.

Eine Hinweistafel für den Jiayuguan-Paß

明成祖朱棣

The Ming Emperor Zhu Di ordered the reconstruction and renovation of the Great Wall, a project that lasted 200 years.

明の成祖朱棣

Portrait de Zhu Di, empereur Chengzu de la dynastie des Ming.

Zhu Di, Kaiser der Ming-Dynastie

明长城　东起辽宁鸭绿江畔、西至甘肃嘉峪关、横跨七个省、市、自治区，长约一万二千七百余华里、故称 "万里长城"。

The Ming Dynasty Great Wall stretches from the Yalu River in the east to Jiayuguan Pass in the west, traveling over 6,300 kilometers.

明代の長城　東は鴨緑江から西は嘉峪関まで、七つの省・市・自治区にまたがり、全長１２７００余華里で、万里の長城と称した。

La **Grande Muraille des Ming.** Elle part à l'est du fleuve Yalu dans la province du Liaoning et se termine à l'ouest à la Passe Jiayuguan dans la province du Gansu, après avoir traversé sept provinces sur une longueur totale de 12 700 lis (6 350 km). D'où son appellation de «Grande Muraille de 10 000 lis».

Die Große Mauer aus der Ming-Dynastie, ca. 12 700 Li (ca. 6350 km) lang

山海关　山海关关城建于公元十二世纪中期，是华北通往东北的咽喉要地，为万里长城第一关，城高25.7米，周长4363.5米，现仅存东墙东门；门上建有两层箭楼，箭楼正中挂有"天下第一关"五个大字匾额，系明代进士萧显所书。

Shanhaiguan Pass was built in the mid 12th century and was of strategic importance for the defense of the northeast. The fortifications at the pass are 25.7 meters high and extend 4,363.5 meters. The far eastern gate through the fortifications is a two-story tower. The plaque over the gate reads, "The First Pass under Heaven". The legend of Meng Jiangnu is sometimes related with Shanhaiguan and at other times with Badaling. The legend tells of how Meng Jiangnu sought out her husband, a conscripted laborer, at the Great Wall. When she found that he had been killed and buried with the soil and gravel used to fill the wall, she collapsed at the base of the wall and cried pitifully. Her anguish was so powerful the wall collapsed and the remains of her husband fell to the ground beside her. A temple was been built near Shanhaiguan to honor Meng Jiangnu.

山海関　山海関の関城は西暦１２世紀の中葉に建てられ、華北地区から東北地区へ通ずる要衝で、万里の長城以北に入る第一の関所となっている。城壁の高さは２５．７

メートル、周辺の長さは４３６３．５メートルで、現在残っているものは城門の東部である。城門の上に二階建てのやぐらがあり、やぐらの中央部にある"天下第一関"の横額は明代の進士である蕭顕の真筆によるものである。

Passe Shanhaiguan. Construite au milieu du XIIe siècle, elle était le passage stratégique entre le Nord et le Nord-Est. Dans cette première passe de la Grande Muraille, d'une hauteur de 25,7 m et d'un périmètre de 4 363,5 m, il ne reste aujourd'hui que l'entrée de l'est, surmontée d'une tour à deux étages à laquelle est suspendue une tablette portant une inscription: «Première passe sous le ciel».

Der Shanhaiguan-Paß Die Festung wurde Mitte des 12. Jahrhunderts gebaut. Sie stellte das Nadelöhr zwischen Nordchina und Nordostchina dar und wird noch heute als der erste Paß der Großen Mauer angesehen. Der 25,7 m hohe Turm hat einen Umfang von 4363,5 m. An der Ostwand befindet sich das einzige gut erhaltene Osttor, dem ein zweistöckiger Wachturm mit Schießscharten folgt. Eine Tafel mit der Inschrift: „Erster Paß unter dem Himmel" hängt in der Mitte des Wachturms und wurde von Xiao Xian aus der Ming-Dynastie geschrieben.

老龙头长城　距山海关城南五公里，是明代蓟镇总兵戚继光为防海盗从山海关长城延伸到此的入海防御工事，建于明嘉靖年间（公元1522-1566年）。它的前部入海如龙头戏水，故称"老龙头"。

"The Old Dragon Head" is five kilometers from Shanhaiguan Pass and was built between 1522 and 1566 by the famous Ming commander Qi Jiguang. The Great Wall has been likened to a dragon, with this being where the dragon's head dips to drink from the waters of the Bohai Sea.

老竜頭長城　山海関の関城の南部から５キロほど離れている。明の名将である戚継光は海賊の侵入を防ぐために、山海関の関城を結びつけ、それをさらに延長し、海上軍事防御施設の築造に取り組んだ。老竜頭長城は明の嘉靖皇帝（西暦１５２２年～西暦

１５６６年）につくられ、その前端は海の中に入っており、竜が大波の中で戯れているようだ。それゆえに「老竜頭」と呼ばれている。

La section de Laolongtou de la Grande Muraille. Située à 5 km de Shanhaiguan, elle fut construite sous le règne de l'empereur Jiajing des Ming (1522-1566) sous la direction du général Qi Jiguang. Ce tronçon se prolonge jusqu'à la mer pour entraver les attaques des pirates.

Der Große Mauerabschnitt in Laolongtou Er liegt 5 km südlich von Shanhaiguan entfernt und ist ein Teil der Großen Mauer bei Shanhaiguan, die von Qi Jiguang, einem Ming-General, zur Abwehr gegen japanische Seeräuber bis ins Meer verlängert worden war.

金山岭长城　地处北京密云县和河北省滦平县交界地带，全长13公里；设敌楼90余座，平均每100米一座，均为二层，式样各异。在城墙以北的制高点上，建有烽火台。它以地形复杂、地势险要、筑城精美而着著；在建筑艺术上能与八达岭长城媲美。

The Jinshanling section of the Great Wall at Jinshanling is situated between Miyun County of Beijing and Luanping County of Hebei Province. Along the 13 kilometers of this section, 90 two-story watchtowers are set at an average of 100 meters apart. At vantage-points to the north of the wall, beacon towers where erected as an early-warning system. The mountains in the area are very steep and precipitous. The positioning of the wall along the steep ridges creates an awe-inspiring scene.

金山嶺長城　北京密雲県と河北省滦平県が境を接しているところにあり、全長１３キロで、城壁の上に９０余りの敵楼（敵の動きを見張る望楼）がある。敵楼は１００メートルの間隔で築かれ、いずれも二階建てのもので、建築構造はまちまちである。城壁の北側の最高地点にのろし台がある。金山嶺長城は複雑な地形、険しい地勢に沿って築かれ、精巧で美しい構造の敵楼があり、建築面での価値は八達嶺長城と同じである。

La section de Jinshanling de la Grande Muraille. Elle se trouve aux confins du district de Miyun à Beijing et du district de Luanping, province du Hebei. Longue de 13 km, elle compte plus de 90 tours de guet à deux étages, de diverses formes. Une terrasse de feu d'alarme fut construite sur la position dominante. Ce tronçon de la muraille est renommé pour son relief varié, son accès difficile et son architecture excellente.

Die Große Mauer in Jinshanling liegt im Grenzgebiet zwischen dem Kreis Miyun, Beijing, und dem Kreis Luanping in der Provinz Hebei. Die Mauer wurde hier auf schwer passierbaren und strategisch bedeutsamen Bergkämmen gebaut. Auf ihrer insgesamt 13 km Länge stehen über 90 zweistöckige unterschiedliche Wachtürme. Auf der Höhe nördlich von der Mauer befindet sich ein Alarmfeuerturm. Hinsichtlich der Baukunst kann sich dieser Abschnitt mit dem bei Badaling messen.

慕田峪西段长城　慕田峪长城经由北京怀柔县西北，西接昌平居庸关，东连密云古北口，是万里长城精华地段。

The Mutianyu section of the Great Wall is located in the northwest of Huairou County in Beijing. To the west is Juyongguan Pass in Changping County and to the east is the Gubeikou Gateway in Miyun County. Along with Badaling and Jinshanling, Mutianyu is one of the most popular sections of rebuilt wall among tourists.

慕田峪長城　北京懐柔県の西北部にあり、西は昌平県の居庸関に接し、東は密雲県の古北口に連なり、万里の長城の粋ともいえる区間である。

La section de Mutianyu de la Grande Muraille. C'est un tronçon de meilleure construction qui relie à l'ouest à la Passe Juyongguan dans le district de Changping, et à l'est à la Passe Gubeikou dans le district de Miyun, traversant le district de Huairou.

Die westliche Strecke der Großen Mauer in Mutianyu Sie erstreckt sich vom Nordwesten des Kreises Huairou bis zur Juyongguan-Festung in Changping im Westen und ist im Osten mit Gubeikou im Kreis Miyun verbunden. Sie ist hier eine sehr imposante Erscheinung.

山西省五台山　乃中国四大佛教圣地之一。五台山上龙泉寺以山门外精美的汉白玉石碑楼雕刻而闻名。
大同云岗石窟　东西长一公里，现有洞窟53个，佛像5100尊。长城要塞助马堡就在它顶部。因为此地长城以黄土杂红土夯筑而成，墙体呈紫色，故称"紫塞长城"。

Mount Wutai in Shanxi Province is sacred to followers of Buddhism. **The Longquan Temple** is located on Mount Wutai and is known for its startling sculptures on the white marble gateway.
The Yungang Grottoes at Datong stretch along one kilometer of cliffs. The construction began around 460 in the Northern Wei Dynasty. At that time, Emperor Wencheng, a devout Buddhist, accepted the suggestion of the eminent monk Tan Yao and ordered the grottoes to be created. The images differ somewhat from the earlier sculptures at the Mogao Grottoes and are the earliest examples of stone Buddhist carvings in China. Some 53 grottoes house over 5,100 Buddhist images, the largest being seventy meters tall and the smallest only two centimeters. The Zhumapu section of the Great Wall passes through the mountains above the grottoes.
The Zisai Great Wall was built by packing the loess soil and covering the resulting mound with firm soil.

山西省の五台山　中国四大仏教の聖地の一つと称されている。山の頂上に竜泉寺があり、寺の表門にある精巧で美しい白い石で造られた石碑がもっとも有名である。大同

雲崗石窟は東西の長さが1キロで、その中に53余りの洞窟、仏像5100基がある。長城の要塞である助馬堡は大同雲崗石窟の上に築かれている。この長城は、黄土や赤土を打ち固めて築いたものである。それゆえに「紫塞長城」と呼ばれている。

Mont Wutai au Shanxi qui est l'un des quatre célèbres monts bouddhiques en Chine. Le temple de la Source du dragon dans le mont est reconnu pour ses sculptures fines sur marbres blancs.
Les Grottes de Yungang à Datong qui s'étend sur un kilomètre. Cet ensemble se compose de 53 grottes dans lesquelles il y a 5100 statues de Bouddha. La forteresse de Zhumapu de la Grande Muraille se situe au-dessus des grottes. Ce tronçon de la Grande Muraille est appelé «Grande Muraille pourpre», parce qu'elle fut construite de terre jaune et rouge.

Der Wutai-Berg in der Provinz Shanxi, einer der vier großen heiligen Stätten des Buddhismus in China. Das Longquan-Kloster auf dem Wutai-Berg ist für seinen fein geschnitzten Ehrenbogen aus Marmor vor dem Eingang bekannt.
Die Yungang-Grotten in Datong verteilen sich innerhalb von 1000 m von Ost nach West. Insgesamt sind 53 Grotten und 5100 Buddhastatuen zu besichtigen. Die Festung Zhumapu liegt außerhalb der Grotten. Die Mauer wurde hier aus Löß und rotem Lehmboden gebaut und erhielt dadurch einen purpurnen Anstrich. Deshalb nennt man diesen Abschnitt „Große Mauer mit purpurnen Festungen".

五台山　　Mount Wutai　　Mont Wutai　　Wutai-Berg

龙泉寺　　　　竜泉寺
The Longquan Temple　　Temple de la Source du dragon　　Longquan-Kloster

云冈石窟　▶
The Giant Buddha at the Yungang Grottoes in Datong
雲崗石窟
Grotte de Yungang
Yungang-Grotten

成吉思汗 （1162–1227）
蒙古汗国大汗。

Genghis Khan (1162-1227) established the great Mongol Empire. His grandson, Kublai Khan, continued his grandfather's conquests by invading China and founding the Yuan Dynasty.

ジンギスカーン （1162 年～ 1227 年）
蒙古汗国の可汗

Genghis Khan (1162-1227) du Khanat mongol.

Chenghis Khan (1162-1227)

西口明长城　出了西口、长城进入内蒙古自治区。在茫茫草原上、牧民以放牧为生、他们勇敢、善骑射。赛马是他们经常举行的活动。

The Ming Dynasty Great Wall stretches from Xikou in Youyu County of Shanxi Province into the Inner Mongolia Autonomous Region. Long the home of nomadic herders, the untamed grasslands continue to witness the equestrian sports of the local horsemen.

西口の明代の長城　西口に出て内蒙古自治区に入る。茫々たる草原で、牧畜民たちは遊牧の生活を送っている。勇敢で狩りをすることに長じている。競馬は日頃よくおこなわれる行事である。

La **Grande Muraille des Ming à Xikou.** Sortant de Xikou, on entre dans la région autonome de Mongolie intérieure. Les Mongols nomades courageux organisent souvent la course à cheval.

Die Große Mauer aus der Ming-Dynastie bei Xikou　Von Xikou aus schlängelt sich die Große Mauer ins Autonome Gebiet Innere Mongolei. Auch heute noch beeindrucken mongolische Hirten durch exzellente Schieß- und Reitkünste.

成吉思汗陵
The Mausoleum of Genghis Khan.
ジンギスカーンの陵

Tombeau de Genghis Khan.
Das Mausoleum von Chenghis Khan

万里长城在陕西榆林县盘亘200余公里、建有烟墩210座、如今已断墙颓垣。

The section of the wall passing through Yulin County in Shaanxi Province has 210 beacon towers along its 200-kilometer length. After centuries of attack by the shifting sands, only the towers rising from the dunes attest to the course of the wall through the desert.

陕西省榆林県内にある長城の長さは２００余キロで、２００余キロの防御線に２１０余りののろし台がある。写真は、明代長城の遺跡。

La section de la Grande Muraille dans le district de Yulin s'étendait sur 200 km et avait 210 terrasses de guet. Il n'existe plus aujourd'hui.

Die Große Mauer schlängelt sich im Kreis Yulin auf einer Strecke von mehr als 200 km. Auf diesem Mauerabschnitt wurden 210 Alarmfeuertürme errichtet. Davon zeugen heute nur noch ein paar Ruinen.

陕西境内的明长城　是1474年在秦长城的遗址上重建起来的。它东起黄河岸边府谷县、西至定边县花马池、全长885公里、史称"秦塞长城"。它历经六百年沧桑、已在沙海中所存无几。然而在米脂的一个小山村里、仍遗留下它的古城堡。

In 1474, work began on restoring the ruins of the Qin Dynasty Great Wall in Shaanxi Province. This section begins at the east bank of the Yellow River in Fugu County and travels to Huamachi in Dingbian County. This 885-kilometer section is known as the Qinsai Great Wall. After 600 years of being constantly buffeted by winds and sand, little remains of the once-great wall through the desert. This castle in a mountain village of Mizhi County attests to the earlier grandeur of this section of the wall.

陕西省内にある明代の長城　西暦１４７４年、秦の長城の遺址を利用して築いたものである。東は黄河の岸辺の府谷県から西は定辺県の花馬池までで、全長８８５キロもあり、歴史学者はそれを「秦塞長城」と呼んでいる。この長城は６００余年の歳月の流れを経てきたが、米脂県にある小さな村で古いとりでの遺跡が発見されている。

La **Grande Muraille des Ming au Shaanxi.** Cette section depuis le district de Fugu à l'est jusqu'au district de Dingbian à l'ouest, d'une longueur de 885 km, fut reconstruite en 1474 sur les ruines de la Grande Muraille des Qin. Elle n'existe plus. On n'a découvert aujourd'hui que les ruines de son fort dans un village dans le district de Mizhi.

Die Große Mauer der Ming-Dynastie in der Provinz Shaanxi Sie wurde auf den Ruinen der Mauer der Qin-Dynastie erbaut. Sie ist 885 km lang. In der Geschichte wurde sie als „Große Mauer auf den Ruinen der Qin-Festungen" bezeichnet. Innerhalb einer Periode von 600 Jahren haben der feine Sand und der Wind die Mauern langsam zerstört. In einem Dorf des Kreises Mizhi befinden sich Überreste einer Festung.

秦始皇陵兵马俑葬坑

Emperor Qin Shi Huang, who first ordered the scattered warlord defensive walls joined as one Great Wall shortly after he founded the Qin Dynasty, was buried in an impressive mausoleum that included an entire army of life-sized Terra Cotta warriors, horses, and weapons.

秦の始皇帝陵の兵馬俑坑

Les statues de guerriers et de chevaux exhumées dans le tombeau de l'empereur Shihuangdi des Qin.

Die Terrakottakrieger und -pferde aus dem Mausoleum von Qin Shi Huang, Xi'an

宁夏同心县明代长城烽火台　明代在宁夏平原修筑长城1500公里。长城纵横在贺兰山脉和黄河之间，扼住蒙古草原至宁夏平原的通道。然而明王朝还是担心蒙古游牧民族侵犯，又在宁夏南部高原设立固原镇，筑第二道长城防线、称为内长城。同心县是固原镇的前哨，同心失宁、固原难保、中原危急。

The region between the Helan Mountains and the Yellow River offered easy access to the Central Plains from the Mongolian grasslands. Therefore, during the Ming Dynasty, 1,500 kilometers of earlier walls were reinforced. Beacon towers in Tongxin County of the Ningxia Hui Autonomous Region are all that remain of this section. On the plateau to the south of Guyuan Town in Ningxia, the Ming decided to construct a second stretch of defensive walls. Much of this construction remains today.

寧夏の同心県内にある明代の長城　明王朝は寧夏平原に１５００キロの防御線を築いた。この長城は賀蘭山脈と黄河の間にまたがり、蒙古草原と寧夏平原へ通ずる要路にある。このほか、寧夏南部の高原の最高地点に固原鎮という防御施設があり、内長城と称した。同心県は固原鎮の前哨地帯である。同心県を陥落すると固原鎮および中原地帯が危急存亡の瀬戸際に追いやられる。

Les terrasses de feu d'alarme de la Grande Muraille des Ming dans le district de Tongxin au Ningxia. Sous la dynastie des Ming, pour mettre le pays à l'abri des incursions des peuples nomades mongols, quelque 1 500 km de murailles furent construites sur la plaine du Ningxia entre le mont Helan et le fleuve Jaune, plus tard, la deuxième ligne de défense, autrement dit la muraille intérieure, fut érigée à Guyuan, au sud du Ningxia. Le district de Tongxin en était l'avant-poste.

Die Große Mauer im Kreis Tongxin, Ningxia, aus der Ming-Dynastie　In der Ming-Dynastie wurde auf der Ningxia-Ebene die Große Mauer, die sich zwischen dem Helan-Gebirge und dem Gelben Fluß erstreckt, mit einer Länge von 1500 km erbaut. Da die Herrscher der Ming-Dynastie sich wegen Angriffe der Nomadenstämme große Sorgen machten, legten sie auf dem Plateau im Südningxia eine zweite Große Mauer als weitere Verteidigungslinie an.

固原镇明代长城

A section of the Great Wall in Guyuan Town of the Ningxia Hui Autonomous Region.

写真は、固原鎮の明代の長城

La Grande Muraille des Ming à Guyuan.

Die Große Mauer der Gemeinde Guyuan aus der Ming-Dynastie

乌鞘岭　是通向河西走廊的门户、是汉长城、明长城必经之地。图为乌鞘岭明长城遗址。

Once an important section protecting the Silk Road, all that remains are the ruins of the Wuqiaoling Great Wall.

烏鞘嶺は河西回廊へ通ずる門戸で、漢代の長城、明代の長城の必ず経なければならないルートである。写真は、明代長城の遺跡。

Wuqiaoling était le passage des murailles des Han et des Ming vers le corridor de Hexi, au Gansu. Sur la photo, des ruines de la Grande Muraille des Ming à Wuqiaoling.

Wuqiaoling war der Eingang zum Hexi-Korridor und der einzige Ort, den die Große Mauer der Ming-Dynastie passierte.

嘉峪关日出　明长城进入甘肃境内。甘肃东接陕西，西连新疆，是中原通往西域的要道 — 中外闻名的"丝绸之路"。它又处于战略重要位置，因此历代帝王在这里修筑长城达八千余公里。万里长城西至这里的嘉峪关。嘉峪关关城为35,500平方米、尚保护完好。关城城内有城、城外有壕、大有一夫当关，万夫莫入的气势。明长城虽然到此为终点，然而出了嘉峪关，汉长城仍然伸向茫茫大漠西行。右下图为嘉峪关全景。

Sunrise at Jiayuguan Pass. The Ming Dynasty extended the earlier Great Wall into Gansu Province. To the east were the earlier sections passing through Shaanxi Province and the ancient capital and heartland of the Chinese nation; to the west were Xinjiang and the Western Regions; beyond lay the mysterious foreign lands of Central Asia. The famous Silk Road passed along this same route and linked China with such distant lands as Rome, North Africa, and Arabia. In order to protect passage along the Silk Road and to provide security for the Central Plains, some 8,000 kilometers of Great Wall were constructed in the area. The first pass a traveler along the Silk Road would reach as they approached the heart of the Chinese nation would be Jiayuguan Pass. The 35,500 square meters of fortifications included an inner city and an outer city. The formidable design of the pass gave rise to the saying, "when but one soldier stands his ground, even 10,000 invaders will not be able to pass."

A bird's-eye view of Jiayuguan Pass. A visitor to Jiayuguan Pass may be curious about a single brick set along the frieze at the Western (Chongguan) Gatetower. A legend explains the brick's presence in this way. A builder, Yi Kaizhan, was asked to help in the construction of Jiayuguan. He was very skilled in calculating the amount of materials needed for such a project and how many days would be needed to complete the work. A supervisor, Zhang Buxin, did not believe in Yi's ability. Yi Kaizhan bet that the number of bricks would be accurate. Zhang Buxin said, "You had better add one more brick in case it is not enough. If it is left over, I will put it on the Chongguan Gatetower." Yi agreed to the idea. And when the number of bricks turned out to be exactly as Yi had predicted, there was just the one extra brick remaining. The brick was placed along the frieze of the tower and remains to this day.

嘉峪関の日の出　明代の長城は甘粛省内にまで延長している。甘粛省は東は陝西省に接し、西は新疆ウイグル自治区に連なり、中原から西域へ通ずる要路にある。この一帯が世にその名を馳せた「シルクロード」である。シルクロードは戦略的要地にあり、各王朝が長城の築造に取り組んだ。各王朝のつくった長城の長さを加えると約８０００余キロになる。万里の長城は西は嘉峪関に至る。嘉峪関の関城は、敷地面積が３５５００平方メートル、建築物は今でも完ぺきな形を保っている。関城の城の中にさらに城があり、城の外にざんごうがある。嘉峪関の関城は「ひとりが関所を守れば万人でも攻め落とすことができない」とさえ言われた。明代の長城に接続し、漢代の長城の西部は茫々たる砂漠へとのびている。写真は、嘉峪関の全景。

Lever du soleil de la Passe Jiayuguan. Le Gansu jouxte le Shaanxi à l'est et le Xinjiang à l'ouest, étant ainsi la grande voie de communication reliant la plaine centrale aux régions de l'Ouest, et aussi la célèbre «Route de la Soie». Le Gansu se trouvait en position stratégique. Plus de 8 000 km de murailles furent donc construites sous plusieurs dynasties. La Passe Jiayuguan était le terme de la Grande Muraille des Ming. Cette passe s'étendant sur un terrain de 35 500 m² est bien conservée. Sur la photo à droite en bas, une vue générale de la Passe Jiayuguan.

Der Jiayuguan-Paß bei Sonnenaufgang Die Provinz Gansu, die im Osten mit Shaanxi und im Westen mit Xinjiang verbunden ist, war ein wichtiger Korridor zwischen dem Landesinnern und dem Westen Chinas, d. h., hier verlief ein Teil der im In- und Ausland berühmten Seidenstraße. Da Gansu sich in einer strategisch wichtigen Lage befand, ließen Kaiser aller Dynastien hier eine über 8000 km lange Mauer bauen. Die Große Mauer der Ming-Dynastie endete im Westen am Jiayuguan-Paß. Die Jiayuguan-Festung hat eine Fläche von 35 500 m² und ist bis heute noch recht gut erhalten. Innerhalb der Festung gibt es eine Stadt, außerhalb den Wallgraben. Vom Paß aus erstreckt dann sich die Große Mauer der Han-Dynastie bis in die Wüstenregion hinein.

Die Jiayuguan-Festung

雄伟的京津冀长城

京津冀地处华北平原，是中国南北交通枢纽，是通往东北、蒙古草原和西北地区的咽喉要地。明代建都于北京。皇帝为了社稷和祖陵的安全，十分重视这一地区的长城修建。这段长城外墙通常以砌石垒成，墙内用黄土充填，顶部用方砖铺就；工程浩大、设计精美、建筑坚固、防御设施完备。所以这一段近千公里的长城，是古长城的精华。而北京境内629公里长的长城最为壮观，有城台827座，关口71座；现已开发的有八达岭、慕田峪、金山岭、司马台等旅游点。本画册精选了百余张翼津京图片，由东向西，将古长城的历史、文化、艺术、建筑，展现在游人朋友面前。

Beijing, Tianjin, and Hebei Province are situated along the North China Plain and have historically been vital communication links between the Chinese heartland and the regions farther north, as well as between China and Manchuria, Mongolia, and Central Asia. Beijing was the capital during the Ming Dynasty. In order to protect the capital and also to protect the gravesites of the emperors and the royal family, the fortifications around Beijing were given particular attention. The Ming Great Wall in this area was made of cut-stone exterior shells filled with packed earth and gravel. The battlements were topped with brick. The engineering quality of these sections was far superior to anything that had come before. This may explain why several sections around the capital have survived in better conditions than sections found elsewhere. Some 629 kilometers of the Great Wall at Badaling, Mutianyu, Jinshanling, and Simatai have been reconstructed and opened to visitors. The 827 watchtowers and 71 passes along these sections provide the perfect backdrop for capturing the awe-inspiring grandeur of the Great Wall of China.

This photo album, with over 100 specially selected images, presents the history, culture, art, and engineering of the Great Wall at Beijing, Tianjin, and Hebei Province.

雄大なスケールを誇る京津冀（北京—天津—河北）長城

京津冀（北京—天津—河北）長城は華北平原にあり、中国南北の重要な交通ルートで、東北地区、蒙古草原および西北地方へ通ずる要衝である。明王朝は北京に首都を置いた。皇帝は社稷と祖先の陵の尊厳を守るために、この区間の工事に取り組んだ。この長城は、外側は石を積み上げた壁で囲み、壁の中に黄土や小石を詰め込み、城壁の上部に四角型の磚（れんが）を積んで築いたものである。建築様式が精巧で美しい京津冀長城は堅固な、完ぺきな防衛施設であると言える。この長城の長さは１０００余キロを超え、中国古代の長城の粋で、そのなかの６２９キロの防御線に８２７

余りののろし台、７１余りの関所、要塞がある。現在は、八達嶺城、慕田峪長城、金山嶺城、司馬台長城などが遊覧観光の名勝地となっている。この画集には京津冀長城に関する百枚の写真が収録されており、その歴史、文化、芸術、建築面での貴重な価値を観光客のみなさんに知っていただけるものと思う。

La Grande Muraille d'une beauté imposante. Sur la grande plaine de la Chine du Nord, Beijing, Tianjin et le Hebei constituaient le passage stratégique qui relie la Chine du Centre et du Sud au Nord-Est, au Nord-Ouest et à la Mongolie intérieure. Beijing fut la capitale de plusieurs dynasties dont les Ming. Pour assurer la sécurité du pays et celle des tombeaux impériaux, la Cour impériale des Ming accorda une importance particulière à la construction de murailles près de la capitale. Ainsi, 1 000 km de murs furent construits. Les parements des murs intérieur et extérieur étaient de dalles, l'espace entre eux était rempli de terre et le dessus était fermé par des briques. Ces murailles étaient extrêmement solides et bien équipées d'installations de défense, représentant le meilleur de la Grande Muraille. Le tronçon de Beijing, long de 629 km, se présentait comme le plus imposant avec ses 827 tours de guet et ses 71 passes. Actuellement, les tronçons de Badaling, Mutianyu, Jinshanling et Simatai sont devenus des sites touristiques. Cet album rassemble une centaine de photos prises à Beijing, à Tianjin et au Hebei, qui reflètent l'histoire, la culture, l'art et l'architecture de la Grande Muraille.

Die majestätische Große Mauer bei Beijing, Tianjin und in der Provinz Hebei

Beijing, Tianjin und die Provinz Hebei liegen auf der Nordchinesischen Tiefebene. Sie sind das Nadelöhr zwischen Nord- und Südchina und auch ein Verkehrsknotenpunkt zu Nordostchina, der mongolischen Steppe und Nordwestchina. Um die Sicherheit des Landes und der Ahnengräberstätte zu gewährleisten, widmeten sich die Kaiser der Ming-Dynastie der Restaurierung und dem Ausbau der Großen Mauer in diesem Gebiet. Die Außenwände dieser Mauerabschnitte sind im allgemeinen mit Steinblöcken verkleidet, ihr Kern ist mit Löß gefüllt und ihre Krone mit quadratischen Ziegeln ausgelegt. Die Mauer wurde solide gebaut und mit vollständigen Verteidigungseinrichtungen versehen. Daher ist dieses ca. 1000 km lange Teilstück die Quintessenz der Großen Mauer, vor allem die 629 km lange Mauer bei Beijing gilt als besonders beeindruckend. Hier stehen 827 Wachtürme und 71 Pässe. Heute sind die Abschnitte der Große Mauer wie in Badaling, Jinshanling und Simatai als Ausflugsziele zugänglich gemacht worden. Für den Bildband haben wir über hundert Fotos aus diesem Gebiet ausgewählt, um Touristen und Liebhabern Chinas die Geschichte, Kultur, Kunst und Architektur der alten Großen Mauer vorzustellen.

河北省迁西县潘家口长城

The Panjiakou section of the Great Wall is located in Qianxi County of Hebei Province. A portion of the wall here was submerged by the Panjiakou Reservoir and so dips into the waters in the east and emerges again to continue its journey to the west.

河北省遷西県の潘家口長城

La section de la Grande Muraille à Panjiakou dans le district de Qianxi au Hebei.

Die Große Mauer in Panjiakou im Kreis Qianxi, Provinz Hebei

河北省迁西县潘家口长城敌楼
The remains of a watchtower at Panjiakou.
河北省遷西県の潘家口長城城壁上の敵楼
Tour de guet de la Grande Muraille à
Panjiakou.
Der Wachturm der Großen Mauer bei
Panjiakou

北京平谷县四座楼山上的敌楼　设在北京东部最高的山峰上，海拔1062米，为明代军事要地。

This watchtower on Sizuolou Mountain was set atop the highest peak in the area to the east of Beijing. At 1,062 meters above sea level, the watchtower commanded a strategic position for warning the Ming armies of any approach from the east.

山の頂上に築かれている敵楼　北京平谷県の東部にあり、標高１０６２メートルで、明朝の頃は戦略的要地であった。

Tour de guet sur le mont Sizuolou dans le district de Pinggu dans l'est de Beijing, à 1 062 m d'altitude.

Der Wachturm auf dem Sizoulou-Berg im Kreis Pinggu, Beijing　Der Wachturm liegt auf dem höchsten Gipfel im Osten Beijings, einem strategisch wichtigen Ort in der Ming-Dynastie.

司马台东段长城敌楼内残留的中心室

Most of the watchtowers, such as this one at the Simatai section of the Great Wall in Miyun County outside Beijing, have decayed in the face of nature's onslaught.

写真は、敵楼の遺跡

L'intérieur d'une tour de guet de la Grande Muraille à Simatai.

Ein verfallenes Depot im Wachturm auf der östlichen Strecke der Großen Mauer in Simatai

北京密云县大角峪长城　障墙密集、陡峭险峻。

These block walls at the Dajiaoyu section in Miyun County provided a defensible passageway along steep cliffs. If the wall was breached, the soldiers could maintain the high ground while strategically retreating uphill.

北京密雲県の大角峪長城　大角峪長城のあるところは、あちこちに障壁があり、山が高く地勢が険しい。

La section de Dajiaoyu dans le district de Miyun, construite sur la montagne à pic.

Die Große Mauer in Dajiaoyu im Kreis Miyun, Beijing　Dichte Sperrwände beherrschen einen schroffen Bergrücken

司马台长城天梯　司马台长城横陈在北京密云县境，全长19公里，多处墙体修建在悬崖绝壁之上。天桥、天梯便是这段长城中险要之处。要登天梯得先过天桥。百米天桥最宽0.5米，最窄0.3米，左右是悬崖。过了天桥才登天梯。它长约50米，倾斜约70度，单面墙体，长长地伸向天际。

The Simatai section of the wall is 19 kilometers long and located in Miyun County outside Beijing. Here the wall travels along the ridges of high mountains and, at certain points, along cliffs formed by huge boulders, in which case the builders were able to create an impregnable wall by merely piling up a few layers of bricks. The most distinctive features of this section are perhaps the stone overpass and stairs leading to the Fairy's Tower. The stone overpass bridges the 900-meter-high peaks of Kulong Mountain. It is 100 meters long and has a width varying from less than 40 centimeters to a little over 50 centimeters. It overlooks deep ravines on both sides. The overpass brings one to the Heavenly Stairs, which lie along a mountain trail that is only wide enough for one person. The 30 or more stone stairs have a gradient of 70 degrees and are each 60 to 70 centimeters wide. A slight breeze can threaten to send a person plunging into the ravine.

司馬台長城の天梯（石の階段）　司馬台長城は北京密雲県内にあり、全長１９キロで、険しい山の上に築かれ、天橋、天梯などの景観がある。天橋、天梯はこの長城のもっとも険しいところである。天梯に登るにはまず天橋を渡らなければならない。天橋の長さは百メートル、幅は０．５メートルで、両側は険しい断崖である。

L'échelle céleste de la Grande Muraille à Simatai. Longue de 19 km, la muraille fut construite sur des précipices dans le district de Miyun dans le nord-est de Beijing. Ce tronçon de muraille, d'une longueur de 50 m et d'une inclinaison de 70°, comme une énorme échelle, s'étend vers le ciel.

Unwegsamer Mauerabschnitt, „Himmelsleiter" der Großen Mauer in Simatai　Der 19 km lange Abschnitt der Große Mauer in Simatai führt quer durch den Kreis Miyun, Beijing. Treppenformartig wurden auf den überhängenden Felsen und steilen Bergwänden Wände gebaut. Die „Himmelsbrücke" und „Himmelsleiter" gelten als die schwersten passierbaren und am strategischsten gelegenen Bestandteile der Mauer. Will man die „Himmelsleiter" besteigen, muß man zuerst die „Himmelsbrücke" überwinden. Die Breite der 100 m langen „Himmelsbrücke" beträgt nur 0,5 bis 0,3 m, zu ihrer beiden Seiten fällt eine steile Bergwand ab. Die Länge der „Himmelsleiter" beträgt ca. 50 m und hat einen Neigungsgrad von ca. 70°. Die lange Wand erstreckt sich bis zum Horizont.

司马台长城障墙　建造在陡峭的山峰上，射孔密布。

This barrier wall at Simatai was built to fortify the already daunting mountain peak. The wall includes closely-set embrasures, holes used by archers.

司馬台長城の障壁　険しい山の頂上に築かれ、上部に矢を射るための穴がある。

Le mur-obstacle avec de nombreuses meurtrières à Simatai, construit sur le précipice.

Sperrwände mit zahlreichen Schießscharten im Abschnitt der Großen Mauer in Simatai wurden auf dem Gipfel errichtet.

司马台长城仙女楼和望京楼　传说有一位美丽仙女住过此楼，故名。望京楼是此处最高点。在秋高气爽的秋夜，登楼能望见北京的灯光。两楼相隔百米，单墙连接，两侧是悬崖峭壁，只有最勇敢的人才能从墙上通过。不知中国古人是如何运砖砌墙的。

Fairy Tower and Tower for Viewing the Capital at the Simatai Great Wall. The tower on top of the Heavenly Stairs is said to have been the haunt of a legendary fairy, who once even left an embroidered shoe there. East of the tower is the highest point in the Simatai section — the Tower for Viewing the Capital. From this high vantage-point, the lights of the capital can be seen on a clear night. The 100 meters of wall between the two towers is wide enough for only one person to pass. Only the bravest of Great Wall enthusiasts dare to pass along this stretch. Most are forced to go downhill and climb some 1,000 meters back up to the tower and the next section of the wall.

司馬台長城の仙女楼と望京楼　かつて美しい仙女がここに住んだことがあるという言い伝えがある。望京楼は山の最高地点にある。さわやかな秋の夜に、望京楼に登ると北京の夜景を眺めることができる。仙女楼は望京楼から百メートル隔たったところにあり、両側は断崖である。勇気をふるいおこしてはじめて城楼の門から出て行くことができる。昔の人がいったいどのようにして山の頂上に城壁を築いたのか不思議である。

Tour de fée et **Tour d'observation de la Grande Muraille à Simatai.** On dit qu'une belle fée habitait la Tour de fée. La Tour d'observation se trouve en position la plus haute. Dans la nuit on peut voir ici la lumière des lampes dans la ville de Beijing. Les deux tours sont reliées d'une muraille mince longue de 100 m, à deux côtés de laquelle on voit un abîme sans fond.

Der Feen- und Wangjinglou-Wachturm der Großen Mauer in Simatai　Einer Sage zufolge wohnte eine schöne Fee einmal in diesem Turm, der nach ihr benannt wurde. Der andere Turm, der Wangjinglou-Wachturm, liegt auf dem höchsten Punkt in diesem Gebiet. Bei klarem Wetter im Herbst kann man abends die Lichter von Beijing sehen. Die beiden Türme liegen ca. 100 m voneinander entfernt und sind durch eine einzige enge Wand verbunden. Zu beiden Seiten sind überhängende Felsen und steile Bergwände. Nur die tapfersten Kämpfer verteidigten diesen Mauerabshnitt. Es ist schwer vorstellbar, wie diese Mauer ohne moderne Technik vor Hunderten von Jahren errichtet worden ist.

司马台水库 长城到此被水流东西截断。水库东部有冷泉，西部有热泉 冬天的水库烟雾弥漫，水温约达20度，足可以让人入水沐浴。

An aerial shot of the Simatai Reservoir. The reservoir divides the wall into two sections. The lake is fed in the east by cold surface streams and in the west by subterranean hot springs. This causes the area to be enveloped in a shroud of mist during cool weather. Some parts of the lake have a constant temperature of 20 degrees Celsius, making it attractive to swimmers even in the dead of winter.

司馬台ダム 長城はダムによって切断される形になっている。ダムの東側には冷泉があり、西側には温泉がある。冬になると、ダムの水面には霧が立ちこめている。水温は20℃で、ダムで水泳をたのしむことができる。

Le réservoir de Simatai. La Grande Muraille est coupée par un réservoir à Simatai. À l'est du réservoir il y a une source d'eau froide, et à l'ouest, une source d'eau thermale de 20 ℃.

Der Simatai-Stausee Die Große Mauer wird durch den Simatai-Stausee in zwei Hälften — Ost- und Westabschnitt — abgetrennt. Im Ostteil wie auch im Westteil des Stausees entspringt jeweils eine Quelle. Die im Westteil ist eine heiße Quelle; im Winter liegt fast immer ein Dunst über dem Stausee, denn die Wassertemperatur erreicht ca. 20° C. Bademöglichkeiten sind vorhanden.

金山岭长城　传说跟随明代总兵戚继光（公元1528-1587年）北上的江浙军士，用镇江大、小金山岛名字命名修建在长城上的大、小敌楼，寄托他们的乡思，故名。

The Great Wall at Jinshanling is virtually a museum of the architectural styles of towers from the Ming Dynasty. As many as 67 towers are found within a distance of 10 kilometers. The towers are mostly two-storied and are square, round, oblate or, for those located at the corners, angular. General Qi Jiguang (1528-1587) was tasked with building this section of the wall. His soldiers were primarily conscripts from Jiangsu and Zhejiang provinces. Homesick, the soldiers named two of the watchtowers after Greater Jinshan Island and Lesser Jinshan Island. This is what has given the section its name.

金山嶺長城　明の名将である戚継光（西暦1528年～西暦1587年）に率いられて辺境の要衝を守備していた将兵らが金山嶺長城の上に敵楼を築いたという言い伝えがある。それぞれが自分の望郷の念をこの敵楼に託していた。金山嶺長城の上にある敵楼はいちばん有名である。

La section de la Grande Muraille à Jinshanling. On dit que les soldats d'origine des provinces du Jiangsu et du Zhejiang, dirigés par le général Qi Jiguang (1528-1587), baptisaient les tours de guet des noms de la grande île de Jinshan et de la petite île de Jinshan à Zhenjiang au Jiangsu.

Die Große Mauer bei Jinshanling.　Man sagt, daß Offiziere und Soldaten aus den Provinzen Jiangsu und Zhejiang, die mit dem Ming-General Qi Jiguang (1528-1587) nach Nordchina kamen, nach den kleinen und großen Jinshan-Inseln ihrer Heimat Zhenjiang ihre Wachtürme, die in der Größe variierten, benannten, um ihr Heimweh zum Ausdruck zu bringen.

金山岭长城敌楼内砖地

The interior of a watchtower at Jinshanling.

写真は、敵楼の内部

Le plancher en brique de la tour de guet de la Grande Muraille à Jinshanling.

Ziegelboden in einem Wachturm der Großen Mauer bei Jinshanling

金山岭长城月夜
A moonlit night at the Jinshanling Great Wall.
金山嶺長城の月夜
Vue nocturne de la Grande Muraille à Jinshanling.
Die Große Mauer bei Jinshanling im Mondlicht

金山岭长城雪景

It is extremely cold on the wall in winter, but it is also at its most impressive at this time of the year, when the mountains are covered with snow. This is the Great Wall at

Jinshanling under a light frosting of winter's snow.

金山嶺長城の雪景色

Vue neigeuse de la Grande Muraille à

Jinshanling.

Die Große Mauer bei Jinshanling in Winterpracht

金山岭长城虎皮墙 筑城时就地取材、用当地碎石堆砌成形、墙呈虎皮色。

The base of this section of the wall at Jinshanling was constructed using crushed stones from the local mountains. The effect has been likened to the skin of a tiger, and hence the name "Tiger Skin Wall".

金山嶺長城の城壁 この長城は、現地で破砕した小石を積み上げて築いたものである。城壁の表面はトラの皮のようだ。それゆえに「虎皮墻」と呼ばれている。

La Grande Muraille de couleur de peau de tigre à Jinshanling. Elle fut construite avec des pierres locales.

Die Außenwand der Großen Mauer bei Jinshanling Diese Wand wurde mit lokalen Steinblöcken gemauert und sieht wie Tigerfell aus. Deshalb heißt sie auch „Tigerfellwand".

古北口金山岭长城 古北口位于北京密云县北部，是通往内蒙和东北的重要隘口。一千多年来，一直为兵家必争之地。

There were three passageways between northeastern China and the Mongolian highlands on the one side and Beijing and the Central Plains on the other. These were Shanhaiguan Pass, Juyongguan Pass, and the Gubeikou Gateway. Gubeikou was set between the two passes in today's Miyun County northeast of the capital city. Gubeikou was the site of frequent warfare and was

heavily guarded by the armies of various dynasties from the 7th to the 13th centuries. During the Ming Dynasty, many defensive installations were added and the strength of the garrison was frequently increased. The main fortification no longer exists and much of the wall has collapsed. The Jinshanling and Simatai sections six kilometers to the east of the gateway remain in fairly good shape and portions of these two have been restored and opened to tourists.

古北口長城 古北口は北京密雲県の北部にあり、内蒙古自治区と東北地区へ通ずる重要な交通ルートである。2000余年来、古北口は戦略的な要地であった。

La Grande Muraille à Gubeikou. Elle se trouve dans le nord du district de Miyun. La Passe Gubeikou était un passage important vers la Mongolie intérieure et la Chine du Nord-Est, un point stratégique disputé par les stratèges depuis deux millénaires.

Der Gubeikou-Abschnitt der Großen Mauer bei Jinshanling Gubeikou liegt im Nordteil des Kreises Miyun, Beijing, und ist ein wichtiger Paß, der zu der Inneren Mongolei und Nordostchina führt. Über mehr als zwei 2000 Jahren war es ein strategisch wichtiger Ort.

金山岭长城主段

A key strategic section of the Great Wall at Jinshanling. Because of the rugged topography, watchtowers along this section of the wall are sometimes as little as 100 meters apart.

金山嶺長城

Le tronçon principal de la Grande Muraille à Jinshanling.

Der Hauptabschnitt der Großen Mauer bei Jinshanling

金山岭长城云海

Frequent mists in the lowlands offered approaching armies welcomed cover in the early morning hours, making this a vulnerable region to the northeast of Beijing. For this reason, the Jinshanling section was completed regardless of the immense difficulties related to the rugged terrain.

金山嶺長城の上にただよう雲

Mer de nuages au pied de la Grande Muraille à Jinshanling.

Ein Wolkenmeer verhüllt die Große Mauer bei Jinshanling

金山岭长城库房楼 在这段长城平台上，建筑一座库房、被称为"库房楼"。库房楼砌有障墙，外侧筑有院墙。此楼实为"总台"，即指挥部。

An unusually large watchtower at Jinshanling is known as "Storehouse Tower" because it has a storehouse on its southern terrace. Defensive barriers, a wall in front, and an extra wall 60 meters downhill protect it. Historical records show that the tower was used as the garrison headquarters.

金山嶺長城の城壁上の敵楼 城壁の上に敵楼があり、武器や弾薬の貯蔵に用いられるところであった。

Tour de dépôt de la Grande Muraille à Jinshanling. Elle était en réalité un poste de commandement.

Der Lagerturm der Großen Mauer bei Jinshanling Auf der Terrasse der Großen Mauer wurde ein Lagerhaus gebaut und als „Lagerturm" bezeichnet. Er hat im Gegensatz zu den anderen Türmen keine Sperrwand, aber an seiner Außenseite wurde eine Hofwand gebaut. In der Tat war er der Hauptturm, nämlich die Kommandostelle dieses Mauerabschnitts.

金山岭长城刀把楼

The watchtowers found at frequent intervals along the Jinshanling section were constructed in a variety of shapes. However, their functions were fairly standard. The lower floors would provide lodgings for the soldiers and were also used for the storage of food and fodder, arms and gunpowder. The upper floors had crenels and embrasures used for keeping watch and for firing weapons at an approaching enemy.

金山嶺長城の城壁上の刀把楼 （城楼の形が刀のつかのようだからこういうふうに称された）

Tour en forme de manche de sabre de la Grande Muraille à Jinshanling.

Der Messergriff-Wachturm der Großen Mauer bei Jinshanling

古北口长城上的圆敌台
A round battle platform near the Gubeikou Gateway. The embrasures, windows through which arrows could be released, are still visible along the top level of the platform.

古北口長城の城壁上の円型ののろし台

Tour de guet ronde de la Grande Muraille à Gubeikou.

Der runde Wachturm der Großen Mauer in Gubeikou

密云水库五座楼山上的三眼敌楼

A fairly typical beacon tower, this tower is on Wuzuolou Mountain near the Miyun Reservoir.

敵楼　密雲県内にある。上部に矢を射るための狭間と窓がある。

Tour avec trois meurtrières, située sur la montagne Wuzuolou, au bord du réservoir de Miyun.

Der Wachturm mit drei Beobachtungslöchern auf dem Wuzuolou-Berg am Miyun-Stausee

密云水库西山顶长城上的古砌圆敌台

An unusual round, stone watchtower on the western hills overlooking the Miyun Reservoir. Since the Miyun Reservoir is a modern addition to the land north of Beijing, this tower would have provided a commanding view of the sprawling river valley.

石を積み上げて築いた円型ののろし台

Terrasse de guet ronde de pierre de la Grande Muraille au bord du réservoir de Miyun.

Der runde Wachturm aus Steinblöcken auf der Großen Mauer im Xishan-Berg am Miyun-Stausee

慕田峪长城　位于北京怀柔县西北、西接居庸关、是万里长城壮观处之一。此地长城的建筑特点是双边垛口，可同时设置滚木擂石，难攻易守。

The Great Wall at Mutianyu is located in the northwest of Huairou County, to the east of Juyongguan Pass. Its construction is unusual in that the embattlements face both directions. Although there is no clear explanation in historical records or an obvious strategic value to this construction, it has resulted in some of the most durable sections of the Ming Dynasty wall.

慕田峪長城　北京懐柔県の西北部にあり、西は居庸関に接し、万里の長城の中でもきわめて壮観なところである。この長城の建築面での特色は、両側にある城壁の上部に矢を射るための垛口（城壁を強化して厚くなった部分）があることで、防御の面で役割を果たした。

La section de la Grande Muraille à Mutianyu. Située au nord-ouest du district de Huairou, à Beijing, et reliée à l'ouest à la Passe Juyongguan, est l'un des tronçons les plus imposants de la Grande Muraille.

Die Große Mauer bei Mutianyu　Sie liegt im Nordwesten des Kreises Huairou, Beijing, und ist im Westen mit der Juyongguan-Festung verbunden. Dieser Mauerabschnitt ist einer der imposantesten Anblicke der Großen Mauer. Die Besonderheiten seiner Baukonstruktion sind die Zinnen, die an beiden Wandseiten angebracht worden sind. Sie dienten der Verteidigung und erleichterten die Abwehr des Feindes.

慕田峪长城全景
The Great Wall at Mutianyu.
慕田峪長城の全景
Vue d'ensemble de la Grande Muraille à Mutianyu.
Panorama von der Großen Mauer bei Mutianyu

怀柔境内响水湖长城

The Xiangshuihu section of the wall in Huairou County was built along steep ridgelines and mountain crests, making this stretch very easy to defend, but extremely difficult to maintain.

懐柔県内にある響水湖長城

La section de Xiangshuihu dans le district de Huairou.

Der Mauerabschnitt am Xiangshuihu-See im Kreis Huairou

慕田峪长城关楼　即正关台关楼。关楼总口处设有三座并列空心敌楼，构造奇特。

The construction of the Mutianyu Pass is quite unusual. Possibly because Mutianyu served primarily as a military pass and allowed only limited civilian traffic, the pass is constructed less like a fortified city and more like a mountain stronghold. Three watchtowers and an embattlement with five embrasures protect the principal entrance.

慕田峪長城の関楼　関楼は三つ並んだ中空の敵楼からなり、建築構造がユニークである。

Passe Mutianyu, autrement dit la Passe Zhengguantai. Trois tours de guet creuses la surmontent.

Der Wachturm der Hauptpaßterrasse bei Mutianyu. Er wird von drei Hohlwachtürmen flankiert.

慕田峪长城　总长2250米，海拔535米，缆车可直通最高点，是北京境内第二个长城游览区。

Some 2,250 meters of the Great Wall have been reconstructed at Mutianyu. Since the difference in elevation between the base of the mountain pass and the highest point on the reconstructed wall is 535 meters, a cable car has been installed to carry visitors up the mountain.

慕田峪長城　全長2250メートル、標高535メートルで、ケーブルカーで山の最高地点まで行ける。現在、慕田峪長城は北京懐柔県の名勝地となっている。

La Grande Muraille à Mutianyu, longue de 2 250 m, à 535 m d'altitude, et équipée de téléphériques, est le deuxième site touristique de la Grande Muraille à Beijing.

Die Große Mauer bei Mutianyu　Sie ist insgesamt 2250 m lang und liegt 535 m über dem Meeresspiegel. Man kann per Seilbahn oder zu Fuß ihre Spitze erreichen. Sie ist der zweite Mauerabschnitt Beijings, der für Touristen zugänglich gemacht worden ist.

慕田峪长城正北楼晚霞

The setting sun silhouettes a watchtower along the northernmost section of the Mutianyu Great Wall.

慕田峪長城の夕やけ

Les nuages crépusculaires de la Grande Muraille à Mutianyu.

Der Wachturm im Norden der Großen Mauer bei Mutianyu in der Abendröte

牛犄角边落日　慕田峪长城依山势迂回而上而下、勾勒出一个偌大的牛角形。

The Mutianyu section rises to a 1,000-meter-high peak in the north and then goes back downhill, forming on the back of the hill a triangle that looks like the horn of an ox, hence the name "Ox-horn Wall".

慕田峪長城の落日　慕田峪長城は険しい山の地勢に沿って築かれている。その形はウシの角のようだ。

Le soleil couchant de la Grande Muraille à Mutianyu.

Der Sonnenuntergang am Ochsenhorn
Die Mauer bei Mutianyu verläuft auf den Bergkämmen in Form eines großen Ochsenhorns.

黄花城长城　境内长城10.8公里，位于北京怀柔县北部，距十三陵约15公里，离北京60公里，是保卫京城、守卫皇陵的重要地段。

The Great Wall at Huanghuacheng stretches some 10.8 kilometers through the northern part of Huairou County. Set about 60 kilometers from the capital and only 15 kilometers from the site of the Ming Tombs, this section was considered to be of strategic importance to the Ming Court and was heavily defended.

黄花城長城　全長１０．８キロで、北京懐柔県の北部にあり、明の十三陵から１５キロ、北京市から６０キロ離れている。都へ向う途中の要衝である。

La section de Huanghuacheng. Longue de 10,8 km, elle se trouve dans le nord du district de Huairou, à 15 km des Treize Tombeaux des Ming et à 60 km de Beijing, étant un tronçon important pour la défense de la capitale et des tombeaux impériaux.

Die Große Mauer bei Huanghuacheng

Dieser Abschnitt mit einer Länge von 10,8 km, befindet sich im Nordteil des Kreises Huairou. 15 km von ihm entfernt befinden sich die Dreizehn Gräber der Ming-Kaiser; Beijing ist 60 km von dieser Stelle entfernt. Er war ein wichtiger Schutzwall für die Hauptstadt und die Kaisergrabstätten.

北京怀柔涧口长城　顺山势而建，气势雄伟。

Jiankou, part of the Mutianyu section, runs 3 kilometers from east to west. It remains fairly well preserved. This section of the wall surprises visitors with its sharp peaks and sudden drops that follow the precipitous slopes. One wonders how the builders managed to construct the wall on such difficult terrain.

北京懐柔県の澗口長城　険しい山の地勢に沿って築かれ、雄大壮麗の至りと言えるものである。

La Grande Muraille à Jiankou dans le district de Huairou.

Die Große Mauer bei Jiankou in Huairou, Beijing　Die imposante Mauer wurde entlang dem Bergverlauf gebaut.

澗口长城雪景　　　　　　　▶

Jiankou in winter.

澗口長城の雪景色

Vue neigeuse de la Grande Muraille à Jiankou.

Der Mauerabschnitt bei Jiankou nach einem Schneefall

涧口长城雨后云散　万里长城隐约呈现在群山峻岭之上。

After a chilling rain, the Great Wall at Jiankou emerges from the mists.

雨上がりの澗口長城　雲と霧に包まれた万里の長城

La Grande Muraille après la pluie à Jiankou.

Der Mauerabschnitt bei Jiankou nach einem Regenschauer　Von den Bergwänden zeichnen sich schemenhaft Teile der Mauer ab.

怀柔旺泉峪长城在风雪中屹立
The Great Wall at Wangquanyu in Huairou County has stood against the onslaught of winds and snow.

懐柔県の旺泉峪長城の雪景色

La Grande Muraille enneigée à Wangquanyu dans le district de Huairou.

Die Große Mauer bei Wangquanyu, Huairou, trotzt heftigen Schneefall

旺泉峪长城上修有三个哨屋的大敌楼

A sentry house situated atop a watchtower at Wangquanyu.

旺谷峪長城の城壁上の敵楼。敵楼の上に三つの偵察所がある。

Grande tour de guet avec trois pièces de la Grande Muraille à Wangquanyu.

Der große Wachturm mit drei Wächterhäusern auf der Großen Mauer bei Wangquanyu

旺泉峪长城上的残破敌楼

Most of the ancient embattlements at Wangquanyu are only ruins today.

写真は、敵楼の遺跡。

Tour de guet délabrée de la Grande Muraille à Wangquanyu.

Ein verfallener Wachturm der Großen Mauer bei Wangquanyu

怀柔松树顶长城　为加强防御能力，长城到此分为内、外长城。内长城通往八达岭、河北涞源，外长城伸向张家口。

The Great Wall at Songshuding in Huairou County. In order to provide additional protection for the capital city during the Ming Dynasty, the wall here forked off into the Outer Great Wall and the Inner Great Wall. The former heads generally west to Zhangjiakou, while the latter leads south along the western extremity of the capital city.

懐柔県の松樹頂長城　長城は内長城と外長城の二つの部分に分かれている。

La Grande Muraille à Songshuding dans le district de Huairou. Pour renforcer la défense, on construisit à partir d'ici une muraille intérieure s'étendant vers Badaling à Beijing et Laiyuan au Hebei, et une muraille extérieure vers Zhangjiakou au Hebei.

Die Große Mauer in Songshuding, Huairou Zur Verstärkung der Verteidigungskräfte unterteilte sich die Große Mauer hier in innere und äußere Mauer: die Innere führt nach Badaling und Laiyuan, Hebei; die Äußere erstreckt sich bis nach Zhangjiakou.

怀柔大榛峪长城　耸立在周围最高的山峰上。
The Great Wall at Dazhenyu clings to the ridgeline of the tallest mountains in Huairou County.

懐柔県の大榛峪長城　起伏した山峰の最高

地点に築かれている。
La Grande Muraille à Dazhenyu, construite sur la plus haute montagne dans le district de Huairou.

Die Große Mauer bei Dazhenyu, Huairou, liegt auf dem höchsten Gipfel der umliegenden Berge.

慕田峪涧口长城日出   Lever du soleil à Mutianyu.
Sunrise at Jiankou.   Ein Sonnenaufgang an der Großen Mauer
涧谷長城の日の出   Jiankou bei Mutianyu

48

黄花城长城　为双面垛口、砖石嶙峋起伏、极为壮观。

The Great Wall at Huanghuazheng features double embattlements. The jagged nature of the wall as it rises along steep slopes creates an impressive image.

黄花城長城　両側の城壁の上部に垛口がある。

La Grande Muraille crénelée en brique et en pierre à Huanghuacheng.

Die Große Mauer bei Huanghuacheng
Die wellenförmige Mauer mit beiderseitigen Zinnen aus Ziegeln und Steinblöcken sieht sehr majestätisch aus.

旺泉峪长城历经沧桑、又遭雷击、已残破不堪。

After 600 years of standing guard over the mountain valley, this watchtower at Wangquanyu was destroyed when lightning struck the wall.

旺谷峪長城の遺跡

La Grande Muraille ruinée à Wangquanyu.

Der Mauerabschnitt in Wangquanyu ist verwittert und wurde zudem vom Blitz getroffen. Dieser Abschnitt bietet einen bizarren Anblick.

北京境内外长城连接处
The junction of the Inner and Outer sections
of the Great Wall in Beijing.
写真は、内長城と外長城が接するところ。

Le point de rencontre des murailles
intérieure et extérieure à Beijing.
Die Verbindungsstelle der inneren und
äußeren Großen Mauer bei Beijing

延庆水泉沟长城　是守卫皇陵的重要地段。

According to ancient Chinese beliefs, disturbing the graves of ancestors would not only cause the spirits to wander in agony, but could also bring tragedy to their descendents. Therefore, the Ming court placed great emphasis on protecting the site of the imperial tombs. This section of wall at Shuiquangou in Yanqing County was central to the defense of the Ming Tombs.

延慶県の水泉溝長城　この長城は皇帝の陵を守るための重要な防御施設であった。

La section de la Grande Muraille à Shuiquangou dans le district de Yanqing, qui servait à défendre les tombeaux impériaux.

Der Mauerabschnitt in Shuiquangou, Yanqing　Er war ein wichtiger Schutzwall für die Grabstätten der Kaiser.

八达岭长城雪景　八达岭城墙高约7.8米、墙基厚约6.5米、墙顶宽约5.8米、地势险峻、为居庸关外口，是明代京都的重要屏障，为中国最早开发的万里长城旅游景点。

Badaling in winter. The wall at Badaling is 7.8 meters tall, 6.5 meters thick at the base, and 5.8 meters wide at the crenels. Badaling was the outer gate for Juyongguan Pass, which in turn was the gateway to Beijing. This section of the wall was the first to be reconstructed and opened to tourists.

八達嶺長城の雪景色　城壁の高さは平均7．8メートル、幅は基部で6．5メートル、上部で5．8メートル、高所にあって地勢が険しい。都へ通ずる重要な交通ルートである。八達嶺は最初に開放された著名な長城として、多くの内外の観光客に親しまれている。

Vue neigeuse de la Grande Muraille à Badaling. D'une hauteur de 7,8 m et d'une largeur de 5,8 m en haut et de 6,5 m en bas, ce tronçon était l'avant-poste de la Passe Juyongguan et aussi un écran protecteur important de la capitale sous le règne des Ming. Il est le premier site touristique de la Grande Muraille.

Die Große Mauer in Badaling in Winterpracht　Dieser Mauerabschnitt ist ca. 7,8 m hoch, der Mauerfuß ca. 6,5 m breit, die Mauerkrone ca. 5,8 m breit. Er liegt auf einem schwer passierbaren Berg und ist ein Engpaß vor der Juyongguan-Festung. In der Ming-Dynastie war dieser Mauerabschnitt ein wichtiger Schutzwall für die Hauptstadt. Im Neuen China war er die erste Mauerstrecke, die für Touristen zugänglich gemacht worden ist.

八达岭长城落日
Sunset at Badaling.

八達嶺長城の落日

Crépuscule de la Grande Muraille à Badaling.

Sonnenuntergang an der Großen Mauer in Badaling

八达岭长城全景
The reconstructed wall at Badaling. Visitors mount the wall at the ancient fortified gate at right-center and can climb in either direction.

八達嶺長城の全景
Vue d'ensemble de la Grande Muraille à Badaling.

Panorama von der Großen Mauer in Badaling

八达岭长城夜景

Artificial lighting gives the wall at Badaling a nighttime appearance of a stairway to heaven.

八達嶺長城の夜景

Vue nocturne de la Grande Muraille à Badaling

Imposanter Anblick der Großen Mauer in Badaling bei Nacht

八达岭长城垛口　长城靠内一侧砌成女墙，靠外一侧则砌成高二米的垛口。垛口下部留有射孔，是用来射杀来犯敌人的。

Embattlements at Badaling. Unlike the wall at Mutianyu, the Badaling section was constructed with defenses facing only out. The inside of the wall has parapets, while the outside has two-meter high crenels and frequent embrasures.

八達嶺長城の垛口（見張り口）　両側にある城壁の上部に2メートルの垛口があり、垛口の下部に矢を射るための穴がある。

Les créneaux de la Grande Muraille à Badaling. On construisit des parapets du côté intérieur de la muraille et des créneaux du côté extérieur sous lesquels on ouvrit des meurtrières.

Die angestrahlten Zinnen der Großen Mauer in Badaling　Die Innenseite der Passage wurde gemauert, die Außenseite besteht aus zwei Meter hohen Zinnenwänden. Außerdem sind hier auch die Schießscharten angebracht.

八达岭长城砌在山崖上的敌台

A watchtower along the sheer mountain slopes of Badaling.

断崖の頂上に築かれた敵楼

Tours de guet construites sur le précipice à Badaling.

Die Wachtürme der Großen Mauer in Badaling wurden an den Felsenwänden errichtet.

57

修葺后的八达岭长城
The reconstructed Great Wall at Badaling.
修復後の八達嶺長城
La Grande Muraille restaurée à Badaling
Die Große Mauer in Badaling nach
Restaurierungsarbeiten

昌平居庸关长城排洪水门
Drainage sluices were set below the wall at
Juyongguan Pass. The gates allowed water
to pass, but could be closed to stop the ad-
vance of enemy troops.

北京昌平区の居庸関長城の水門（洪水の水
を排出するために、用水路などに設けられ
たゲート）

Passe-déversoirs de la Grande Muraille à
Juyongguan.

Das Hochwasserableitungstor der Großen
Mauer bei Juyongguan in Changping

从过街塔门洞看居庸关关楼

The main gate of Juyongguan Pass as seen through the Cloud Terrace. The Cloud Terrace was built in the Yuan Dynasty. The hexagonal archway, although seemingly unique today, was actually common during the Yuan and Song dynasties. The foundations of the five pagodas of the Ming Dynasty Tai'an Temple are found on top of the terrace.

道路にまたがり下が通路になっている塔の門の下から居庸関の城楼を眺める

Passe Juyongguan.

Blick vom gegenüberliegenden Pagodentor auf den Turm des Juyongguan-Passes

居庸关云台券门浮雕、是元代艺术珍品。

Carved on both sides of the gateway are images from Lamaistic Buddhism, such as the four heavenly kings and six "snares". Buddhist scriptures in Nepalese Sanskrit, Tibetan, Mongolian, Uygur, Han, and Xixia attest to the cultural exchanges between the ethnic groups in China during the Yuan Dynasty.

居庸関の雲台　浮彫と6種類の文字で刻まれた陀羅尼経がある。元代の貴重な芸術品である。

Des reliefs sur la Terrasse des nuages de Juyongguan, sculptés sous la dynastie des Yuan.

Das Relief auf dem Bogen der Wolken-Terrasse in der Juyongguan-Festung ist eine Kuriosität aus der Yuan-Dynastie.

河北怀来县陈家堡长城
The Chenjiapu section of the wall in Huailai
County of Hebei Province.
河北省懐来県の陳家堡長城

La section de Chenjiapu dans le district de
Huailai au Hebei.
Ein Mauerabschnit bei Chenjiapu im Kreis
Huailai, Provinz Hebei

陈家堡长城上的敌楼
A watchtower at Chenjiapu
陳家堡長城の城壁上の敵楼
Tours de guet de la Grande Muraille à
Chenjiapu.
Der Wachturn auf der Großen Mauer bei
Chenjiapu

修缮后的八达岭东段长城
The eastern section of the Great Wall at
Badaling after reconstruction.

修復後の八達嶺長城の東部区間

Le tronçon d'est restauré de la Grande
Muraille à Badaling.

Der östliche Abschnitt der Großen Mauer in
Badaling nach Restaurierungsarbeiten

北京门头沟区黄草梁长城
The Great Wall at Huangcaoliang in the
Mentougou District of Beijing.
北京門頭溝区の黄草梁長城

La Grande Muraille à Huangcaoliang dans
l'arrondissement de Mentougou de Beijing.
Der Mauerabschnitt in Huangcaoliang im
Mentougou-Bezirk, Beijing

河北怀来镇边城村东城门
The east gate at Biancheng Village in Huailai Town of Hebei Province continues to be used every day by local villagers.
河北省懐淶鎮辺城村の東側の城門

L'entrée est de la muraille du village de Biancheng dans le district de Huailai au Hebei.

Das Osttor des Biancheng-Dorfs in der Gemeinde Huailai, Hebei

河北省涞源县杜家台山脊上一串敌楼

The proximity of watchtowers was a reflection of the difficult terrain and the need for increased strength along the wall. This close cluster of watchtowers is along a ridge at Dujiatai in Laiyuan County of Hebei Province.

河北省涞源県の杜家台長城の城壁上の敵楼

Tours de guet de la Grande Muraille à Dujiatai dans le district de Laiyuan au Hebei.

Eine Reihe von Wachtürmen auf dem Dujiatai-Bergrücken im Kreis Laiyuan, Provinz Hebei

河北涞源县乌龙沟长城
The Wulonggou section in Laiyuan County
of Hebei Province.

河北省涞源県の烏竜溝長城

La section de Wulonggou dans le district
de Laiyuan.

Die Große Mauer in Wulonggou im Kreis
Laiyuan, Hebei

河北涞水县马水长城
The Mashui section in Laishui County.
河北省涞水県の馬水長城

La section de Mashui dans le district de
Laishui au Hebei.

Die Große Mauer in Mashui im Kreis Laishui,
Hebei

河北涞源县浮图峪长城
The Futuyu section in Laiyuan County.
河北省涞源県の浮図峪長城

La section de Futuyu dans le district de Laiyuan.
Die Große Mauer bei Futuyu im Kreis Laiyuan, Hebei

沐浴春雨后的浮图峪长城
The Great Wall at Futuyu after a spring rain.
雨上がりの浮図峪長城
La Grande Muraille à Futuyu, après la pluie
printanière.
Die Große Mauer bei Futuyu nach einem
Frühlingsregen

辟邪门兽　雕刻在河北涞源县杜家台长城敌楼的门额上，极为罕见。

This door beast carved over the entrance to a watchtower at Dujiatai was meant to ward off evil spirits.

魔除けのために門の通路の上に刻まれた動物　河北省涞源県の杜家台長城城壁の敵楼の門の通路上に彫刻された動物は中国古代建築史上まれに見るものである。

L'animal de protection contre les démons, sculpté sur la porte de la tour de guet de la Grande Muraille à Dujiatai dans le district de Laiyuan.

Das gemeißelte Torrelief am Wachturm der Großen Mauer bei Dujiatai, Hebei, stellt eine Tierfigur dar, die der Teufelsvertreibung diente.

河北涞源杜家台长城敌楼

A watchtower at the Dujiatai section of the Great Wall.

河北省涞源県の杜家台長城城壁上の敵楼

Tour de guet de la Grande Muraille à Dujiatai.

Ein Wachturm auf der Großen Mauer bei Dujiatai, Hebei

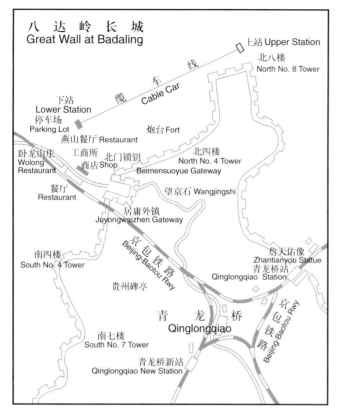

八达岭长城
Great Wall at Badaling

上站 Upper Station
北八楼 North No. 8 Tower
缆车线 Cable Car
下站 Lower Station
停车场 Parking Lot
炮台 Fort
燕山餐厅 Restaurant
卧龙山庄 Wolong Restaurant
工商所商店 Shop
北门锁钥 Beimensuoyue Gateway
北四楼 North No. 4 Tower
餐厅 Restaurant
望京石 Wangjingshi
居庸外镇 Juyongwaizhen Gateway
京包铁路 Beijing-Baotou Rwy
南四楼 South No. 4 Tower
贵州碑亭
詹天佑像 Zhantianyou Statue
青龙桥站 Qinglongqiao Station
南七楼 South No. 7 Tower
青龙桥 Qinglongqiao
京包铁路 Beijing-Baotou Rwy
青龙桥新站 Qinglongqiao New Station

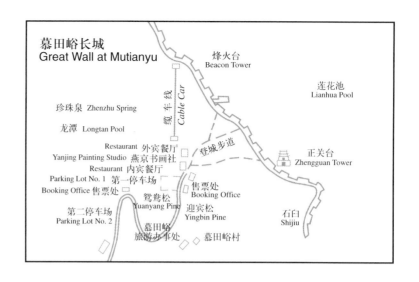

慕田峪长城
Great Wall at Mutianyu

烽火台 Beacon Tower
莲花池 Lianhua Pool
珍珠泉 Zhenzhu Spring
龙潭 Longtan Pool
缆车线 Cable Car
烽城步道
正关台 Zhengguan Tower
Restaurant 外宾餐厅 Yanjing Painting Studio 燕京书画社
Restaurant 内宾餐厅
Parking Lot No. 1 第一停车场
售票处 Booking Office
Booking Office 售票处
鸳鸯松 Yuanyang Pine
迎宾松 Yingbin Pine
石臼 Shijiu
第二停车场 Parking Lot No. 2
慕田峪旅游办事处
慕田峪村

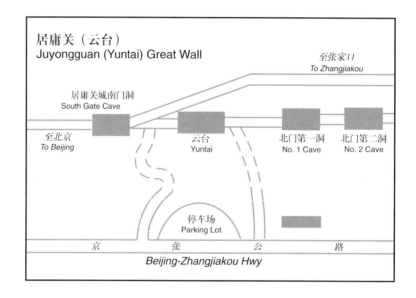

居庸关（云台）
Juyongguan (Yuntai) Great Wall

至张家口 To Zhangjiakou
居庸关城南门洞 South Gate Cave
至北京 To Beijing
云台 Yuntai
北门第一洞 No. 1 Cave
北门第二洞 No. 2 Cave
停车场 Parking Lot
京 张 公 路 Beijing-Zhangjiakou Hwy

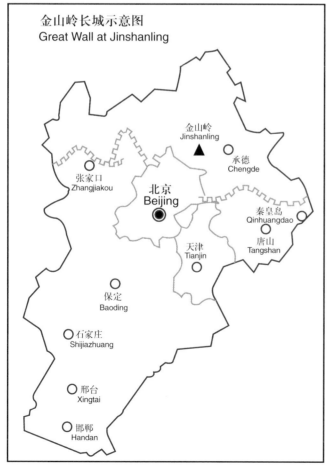

金山岭长城示意图
Great Wall at Jinshanling

金山岭 Jinshanling
承德 Chengde
张家口 Zhangjiakou
北京 Beijing
秦皇岛 Qinhuangdao
天津 Tianjin
唐山 Tangshan
保定 Baoding
石家庄 Shijiazhuang
邢台 Xingtai
邯郸 Handan

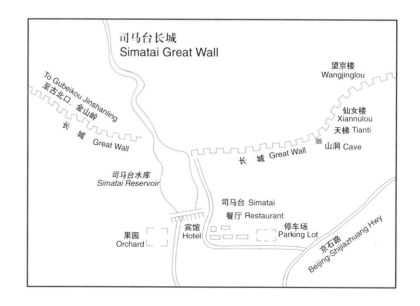

司马台长城
Simatai Great Wall

望京楼 Wangjinglou
仙女楼 Xiannulou
天梯 Tianti
山洞 Cave
To Gubeikou Jinshanling 至古北口、金山岭
长城 Great Wall
长城 Great Wall
司马台水库 Simatai Reservoir
司马台 Simatai
餐厅 Restaurant
宾馆 Hotel
停车场 Parking Lot
果园 Orchard
京石路 Beijing-Shijiazhuang Hwy

我国历史朝代公元对照简表
A Brief Chronology of Chinese History

夏 Xia Dynasty		约前21世纪－约前16世纪	ca. 21c. B.C.－ca. 16c. B.C.
商 Shang Dynasty		约前16世纪－约前1066	ca. 16c. B.C.－ca. 1066 B.C.
周 Zhou Dynasty	西周 Westarn Zhou	约前1066－前771	ca. 1066 B.C.－771 B.C.
	东周 Eastern Zhou	前770－前256	770 B.C.－256 B.C.
	春秋时代 Spring and Autumn Period	前770－前476	770 B.C.－476 B.C.
	战国时代 Warring States Period	前475－前221	475 B.C.－221 B.C.
秦 Qin Dynasty		前221－前206	221 B.C.－206 B.C.
汉 Han Dynasty		前206－公元220	206 B.C.－A.D. 220
魏、晋、南北朝 Wei-Jin period and Northern & Southern Dynasties		220－581	
隋 Sui Dynasty		581－618	
唐 Tang Dynasty		618－907	
五代十国 Five Dynasties/Ten Kingdoms		907－979	
宋 Song Dynasty		960－1279	
辽 Liao Dynasty		916－1125	
西夏 Xixia Dynasty		1038－1227	
金 Jin Dynasty		1115－1234	
元 Yuan Dynasty		1279－1368	
明 Ming Dynasty		1368－1644	
清 Qing Dynasty		1644－1911	